The publisher gratefully acknowledges
the generous contribution of
The MacPherson Charitable Trust,
which helped to make
this RWU Press edition of
Philip Dru: Administrator
a reality.

PHILIP DRU: ADMINISTRATOR

by

EDWARD MANDELL HOUSE

Robert Welch University Press

Appleton, Wisconson

1998

**New 1998 edition with
foreword by William N. Grigg, index,
and selected appendices
not in the original.**

Originally published in 1912.
This printing has been proofread against the 1919
edition, published in New York by B. W. Huebsch.

Published by
Robert Welch University Press
P.O. Box 8050
Appleton, Wisconsin 54913

RWU
PRESS
Robert Welch University Press

Printed in the United States of America
Library of Congress Catalog Card Number: 98-61149
ISBN: 1-892647-00-1

Foreword to the 1998 Edition

Philip Dru: Administrator belongs on the short shelf of political works which are read primarily for precautionary reasons. As with Adolf Hitler's *Mein Kampf*, *Dru* is a dauntingly candid description of one man's ruthless ambition; like the *Communist Manifesto*, *Dru* can be read as a detailed schematic for subversion. The book, which expressed the "ethical and political faith" of a man who came to be known as the "Assistant President of the United States,"[1] — is perhaps best regarded as a successor to Machiavelli's essay *The Prince*: It set forth the designs of an amoral plotter who was the "power behind the throne."

Just as it is impossible to understand the tragedy of modern totalitarianism without some understanding of the hate-drenched scribblings of Hitler and Marx, it is at best very difficult to understand the covert forces that have shaped America's political destiny without some understanding of the fictional Philip Dru and his historical counterpart, "Colonel" Edward Mandell House. Although sixty years have passed since House's death, the changes he wrought upon America's political and economic system remain with us. Although *Dru* can be profitably read for the insights it yields in retrospect, its real value resides in the insights it provides regarding the tactics and objectives of the Power Elite that House represented, which remains firmly in control of America's political culture.

House, an austere figure who was born to a wealthy plantation owner in Houston in 1858, wrote *Dru* anonymously in Austin during a six-week period in late 1911 and early 1912. He explained in a private letter that "Governmental affairs, both domestic and foreign, have been almost my sole interest since boyhood."[2] Although he dropped out of Cornell after one year and was never elected to political office, "Colonel" House arguably did more to reshape American politics, with respect both to domestic and international affairs, than any single figure. Historian Thomas J. Nock of Southern Methodist University refers to House as "one of the first 'Kingmakers' in modern American politics."[3] After writing *Dru*, House — who had enjoyed a very successful career as a political kingmaker in Texas — chose New Jersey Governor Woodrow Wilson to be the vessel of his ambitions.

House was introduced to Wilson on November 24, 1911, shortly before the "Colonel" began writing *Dru*.[4] Arthur Walworth, who edited House's diaries for the Yale University Press, records that at that meeting "a true marriage of minds took place.[4] They found a remarkable congruence in their ideas about men and measures. Afterwards House wrote to his brother-in-law: 'Never before have I found both the man and the opportunity.'"[5] "Almost from the first," House later recalled of Wilson, "our minds vibrated in unison." Prior to meeting Wilson, "I was like a disembodied spirit seeking corporeal form," House reflected. "I found my opportunity in Woodrow Wilson."[6]

Perhaps the most important area of compatibility between House and Wilson was their shared enthusiasm for socialism. House used his fictional surrogate Philip Dru to express a passion for "Socialism as dreamed of by Karl Marx," augmented with "a spiritual leavening." As an academic, Wilson had written that "we ought all to regard ourselves as socialists" and inveighed against "selfish, misguided individualism...."[7] In lectures he taught as a professor of international law at Princeton between 1892 and 1894, Wilson synthesized an internationalism rooted in socialist perspectives with concepts derived from a distortion of Christianity, yielding a Dru-like variety of spiritually leavened Marxism.[8] Like House, Wilson was intoxicated with a sense of his own historical significance. Notes professor Nock: "On his thirty-third birthday, [Wilson] wrote in his 'Confidential Journal' the stunning question: 'Why may not the present generation write, through me, its political autobiography?'"[9]

Dru envisioned nothing less than the abolition of America's constitutional order through a military putsch. Charles Seymour of Yale University, who served with House in a secretive group called the Inquiry and later edited House's intimate papers, observed that "Philip Dru"'s intention was "to remake the mechanism of government" by creating "a new American Constitution, better fitted than the old for the spirit and conditions of the twentieth century."[10] House candidly and frequently expressed his contempt for the U.S. Constitution. "For a long time it had seemed to me that our Government was too complicated in its machinery and that we had outgrown our Constitution," wrote House in 1922. "It has been my constant wonder that our people were willing to go along without protest with such an inefficient machine.... The negative character of our Government and its lack of responsiveness to the will of the people makes it less efficient than it should be.... One of the purposes in writing 'Philip Dru' was a desire to bring to our people a realization of this." House boldly asserted that the vision sketched out in *Dru* represents "a really responsive form of government" that would give the people "as good government as they deserved...."[11] Professor Seymour notes that the House/Wilson/Dru ideology was not American constitutionalism, but rather "social democracy reminiscent of Louis Blanc and the revolutionaries of 1848" — in other words, revolutionary Marxism.

House's fictional alter-ego Philip Dru is a young West Point graduate who leaves the U.S. Army to organize a military revolt against the government of the United States and the Constitutional order it was designed to protect. In typically overripe prose, House (who never served in the military; the title "Colonel" was strictly honorary) describes Dru as a messianic figure who triumphantly arrives in Washington "panoplied in justice and with the light of reason in his eyes ... the advocate of equal opportunity ... with the power to enforce his will." After abolishing the old order, Dru appoints himself "Administrator" — that is, dictator — of the new regime, in which "the property and lives of all [are] now in the keeping of one man." Like Julius Caesar, who accepted the crown amid anguished professions of chaste reluctance, Dru found the powers of a dictator to be "distasteful," but he managed to curb his repugnance.

Having seized totalitarian power, Dru begins to remold American society. He issues a decree making any attempt to restore America's constitutional order "seditious, and ... [punishable] by death." Dru's regime then embarks upon a program of radical social engineering that eerily prefigures both the Wilson Administration's "New Freedom" agenda and FDR's

"New Deal." Observes professor Walworth, Dru "set up a system for social security, and arranged for the representation of labor on corporate boards and for a sharing of profits among the workers. Moreover, he imposed a graduated income tax, and developed a banking system that presaged the Federal Reserve; and he united the Great Powers of the world in a league for collective security."[12] In *Dru*, House described a coalition that presaged the development of the League of Nations, an organization he would himself be instrumental in creating.

Wilson eagerly embraced the *Dru* blueprint. Immediately after his election in 1912, Wilson sought refuge in a cottage in Bermuda "to do a lot of thinking." His meditations were guided by a copy of *Dru*. Professor Walworth points out that "Many of [*Dru*'s] prescriptions for reform ran parallel to those set down in Wilson's *The New Freedom: A Call for the Emancipation of the American People*."[13] That Wilson employed *Dru* as a policy template was attested by Franklin K. Lane, Wilson's Secretary of the Interior, who wrote in a letter to a friend that "All that book has said should come about.... The President comes to Philip Dru in the end."[14]

The anti-constitutional innovations that were brought about during Wilson's tenure — particularly the imposition of the income tax and the Federal Reserve System — were directly derived from *Dru*. Granted, House and Wilson didn't tear down the existing constitutional order through military violence, preferring instead to employ conspiratorial subtlety. House once referred to the "graveyard" secrecy with which he and Wilson plotted their strategy.[15]

Hindsight tends to have a telescoping effect; accordingly, it may be difficult to understand the radical nature of the *Philip Dru* agenda. The arsenal of House and his co-conspirators included ciphers and codes to disguise both written and spoken communications.[16] Of course, they felt no compunctions about lying to the American public regarding their intentions, particularly with respect to key elements of the *Dru* agenda.

To take but one example: As devout socialists, House and Wilson eagerly sought the creation of a central bank. However, Wilson's campaign platform explicitly rejected a central banking plan devised by Republican Senator Nelson Aldrich. No problem, House explained: "The platform says 'We oppose the so called Aldrich plan for the establishment of a central bank.' This does not mean, I take it, that the central banking idea is opposed but that the Aldrich plan for a central bank is opposed."[17] In fact, the Federal Reserve System created during the Wilson Administration, with House's indispensable help, was indistinguishable from the Aldrich plan — and Aldrich himself was among its architects.[18]

House's alter-ego Philip Dru displayed his creator's gift for pious duplicity. Although he inveighs against the monied interests who are conspiring to control the American political system, he sees nothing amiss in bringing those same interests into his government, once he has obtained total power. It will be "the educated and rich, in fact the ones that are now the most selfish, that will be in the vanguard of the procession," Dru explains. "They will be the first to realize the joy of it all, and in this way they will redeem the sins of their ancestors."

Dru creates a ruling directorate in which "corporations share with the government and states a certain part of their net earnings" in exchange for representation in centralized policy-making councils. Dru insisted that "it would be more to the advantage to have business conducted by corporations than by individuals in a private capacity." Accordingly, "The people were asked to curb their prejudice against corporations," House narrates. "It was promised that in the future corporations should be honestly run" — under centralized government direction, of course. In similar fashion, House assembled an oligarchical vanguard that included such mega-bankers as Paul Warburg, Frank Vanderlip, and J.P. Morgan. These powerful representatives of the "Money Power," along with a cadre of 100 "forward-looking" social planners that were called "The Inquiry," helped to create the Council on Foreign Relations (CFR), which since 1921 has served as the ruling directorate for America's Power Elite.

The CFR's creation was necessary, in large measure, because of the failure of House and Wilson to achieve the crowning element of the Philip Dru agenda: The creation of a League of Nations that would unite the world under the reign of a socialist oligarchy. The League did come into existence, but the refusal of the U.S. Senate to ratify U.S. participation in the body left it impotent and largely irrelevant. In a fashion similar to Britain's Fabian Socialists, who pursued the ends of revolutionary socialism through evolutionary means, House and his comrades created the CFR as a means of capturing America's academic, economic, and policy elite, and catechizing it on behalf of socialist internationalism.

Many who are aware of the CFR regard it to be a stuffy but generally respectable institution — a think-tank composed of policy wonks and gray bureaucrats. This description is essentially correct. It is also entirely inadequate. The CFR is the institutional guardian of the Philip Dru vision; its role is to define a ruling "consensus" that is in harmony with that vision — spiritually leavened Marxism, as interpreted by a ruling vanguard of political, academic, media, and corporate leaders. The concise term that describes this philosophy is Fascism.

It was House, not Benito Mussolini, who pioneered the concept of the corporate state. House cheerfully acknowledged that fact in an essay he wrote for *Liberty* magazine shortly after the election of FDR: "In 1911, I wrote a book entitled *Philip Dru: Administrator*. It came in for considerable discussion, favorable and unfavorable. It was, in fact, a semi-political novel showing how a dictator seized the government of the United States and anticipated Mussolini by a number of years."[19] At the time that House offered this admission, Fascism was the collectivist flavor of the month. Mussolini was the darling of both corporate and intellectual elites. Even the leaders of America's "mainline" religious denominations could be found hymning the praises of Fascism: In 1935, Dr. John C. Bennett, president of the Union Theological Seminary, praised Fascism for its "constructive value in a stage of the development of a new economic order."[20]

In an article published in 1935, House wrote a breathtaking apologia for Fascist imperialism in Africa. "The tension in Europe will lead to new disasters unless the imperial urge of Mussolini has the opportunity to spend itself on African soil," declared House. "The legions of Mussolini marching into Africa may lay the foundation for a new Roman Empire great enough to give the Italian people a chance to breathe. If Mussolini succeeds, Italy will expand in Africa without exploding in Europe."[21]

Arguably, Mussolini was even more faithful to the Philip Dru agenda than Wilson and House had been. After seizing power in a *coup de main*, Mussolini — who had been a revolutionary Marxist of the reddest hue — created a corporate state based upon an attenuated vision of socialism that emphasized "spiritual" and "heroic" values, rather than economic egalitarianism. His Fascist credo — "Everything within the state; nothing outside the state; nothing against the state" — was a perfect adaptation of Dru's ruling philosophy. The Fascist regime was nothing if not "responsive" and "efficient"; as was often said, Il Duce made the trains run on time. Even his war against Abyssinia could be looked upon as a regionally adapted version of Dru's war of conquest in Latin America.

Among Mussolini's most devoted admirers was Roosevelt's "Brain Trust," which studied his corporatist state as a model for American reforms.[22] Significantly, the Roosevelt clique turned to Fascism's primary source for guidance as well: House was paid court by FDR, who sought his wisdom regarding foreign policy. The "secret diary" of FDR's chief of staff Harold L. Ickes recorded an Oval Office huddle involving FDR and House on October 18, 1933.[23] In the same source, Ickes also conceded that the Roosevelt Brain Trust was secretly "working toward a society of modified Communism," a near-transliteration of Philip Dru's objective, and a tidy summation of the Fascist vision.[24]

The Philip Dru vision was only partially consummated by Wilson; FDR was much more successful. Writing in July, 1937, Thomas W. Phelps, then Washington Bureau Chief for the *Wall Street Journal*, offered the following remarkable acknowledgment:

"As Congress puts the finishing touches on the legislative program for the first four years of the Roosevelt Administration, Col. E.M. House, confidant of President Roosevelt, emerges as the prophet, if not the real brain trust of the New Deal. Almost 25 years ago, House wrote of a revolution led by a young West Pointer, who triumphed in one brief but bloody battle; became a benevolent dictator and proceeded to reshape the American Government. In its large outlines, almost the entire revolutionary program has been put through or is in process of being realized under two Democratic Presidents who have served since House turned novelist for a few weeks."[25]

Shortly after this celebration of the triumph of Fascism in America, America found itself maneuvered into fighting Fascism as an ally of Stalin's Soviet Union. In short order, House's admissions were cast into the memory hole — along with every copy of *Philip Dru* that the ruling elite could get its hands on.

Columnist Westbrook Pegler, a capable and pugnacious critic of collectivism of all varieties, understood the significance of *Dru* as a totalitarian template. Pegler was among the most outspoken critics of FDR's assault upon the Constitution; he had also issued incandescently critical reviews of Mussolini's regime from Italy at a time when doing so required more than a little courage. Writing in 1954, Pegler informed his readers, in characteristically forthright fashion, that "During all these years since 1911 or 1912, by the secret evil design of one man, the Government of this great republic has been corrupted and transformed into Fascism, which that man invented long before Benito Mussolini was heard of outside his native village. At that time Adolf Hitler was just another country boy in Austria." Pegler described Hitler and Mussolini, as well as Wilson and FDR, as disciples of House.[26]

Despite the efforts of the political elite to suppress the distribution of *Philip Dru* and disavow House's embarrassing admissions, Pegler neglected no opportunity to remind the public of Fascism's real origins. "Wilson's Rasputin, the most influential private citizen in America and indeed one of the most powerful human beings in all the world, copyrighted Fascism at a time when Mussolini was just a loud-mouthed, hand-to-mouth Communist in Milan, [and] Lenin and Trotsky were unknown vermin hiding in dark corners of Geneva and New York," noted Pegler in a typical column. [27]

For Pegler, writing at a time when the Congressional Reece Committee was investigating the underpinning and actions of the "Invisible Government" assembled by House and his co-conspirators, *Philip Dru: Administrator* was among the most valuable pieces of evidence in the effort to prove that

America's descent into collectivism was the product of pre-meditated conspiracy, rather than the impersonal labors of indifferent historical forces. "[E]ven today few citizens have heard of [Philip Dru] and hardly one in a million has read it," he noted. "And, of course, the press will still ignore it diligently.... Practically all our historians and our teaching professors either know nothing about all this or refuse to teach this historical information to their students. One of the most important political documents of our age has been blacked out."[28]

That political document is now available in a reissued edition, and it remains just as timely today. This is not because of its deathless prose or its vibrant characterizations; indeed, there is hardly a page that can be read without embarrassment for the author's ineptitude. The reader sufficiently diligent to plow through House's congealed prose will be rewarded. Crucial descriptions of House's malignant philosophy are embedded in rambling soliloquies and used to season improbable heart-to-heart talks between Dru and his inamorata, Gloria Strawn. In Chapter VI, "The Prophet of a New Day," the full scope of House's messianic delusions is revealed, as is his devotion to spiritualized Marxism. Chapters XIX-XXIV describe Dru's military putsch. The remainder of the book presents a detailed outline of the Dru/House agenda, and the necessary institutions to bring that agenda to fruition. The political elite House represented is busily employing the ruling instruments that represent Philip Dru's vision — the United Nations, the Breton Woods financial institutions, the Federal Reserve, the CFR and its kindred councils — to carry out the ongoing drive to create a new world order. Domestically, "public-private partnerships" remain in vogue — corporatist mechanisms drawn from House's Fascist model. House's vision of a "responsive" and "efficient" government unfettered by constitutional limitations is shared with near unanimity by the political elite and the media's opinion cartel. And throughout the world — whether in the U.S., Latin America, the European Union, the Former Soviet Union, or Red China — there is a definable trend toward the acceptance of House's modified Marxism as the dominant political and economic philosophy, as House's disciples pursue the global triumph of his vision in "graveyard silence."

Philip Dru: Administrator is arguably the most influential political tract of the twentieth century. Its influence has been written in blood and paid for in the coin of stolen liberties. But its malignant vision has not yet triumphed completely. Those who would defeat the designs of the Power Elite must first understand those designs — and they are on full display in *Philip Dru.*

William Norman Grigg
Appleton, Wisconsin
September 1998

Footnotes to the Foreword

1. *Boston Transcript*, February 22, 1915, as quoted in the diary of Edward Mandell House (hereafter "Diary") for February 18, 1915.
2. Ibid.
3. Thomas J. Nock, *To End All Wars: Woodrow Wilson and the Quest for a New World Order* (Princeton, New Jersey: Princeton University Press, 1992), pg. 20.
4. Ray Stannard Baker, *Woodrow Wilson: Life and Letters*; *Vol. Three, Governor 1910-1913* (Garden City, New York: Doubleday, 1931), p. 294.
5. Walworth, pg. 7.
6. Nock, pp. 20-21.
7. Nock, p. 7.
8. Nock, p. 8.
9. Nock, p. 13.
10. Charles Seymour, *The Intimate Papers of Colonel House*, *Vol. 1* (Boston and New York: Houghton Mifflin Company, 1926-28), 152-153.
11. House, letter of July 10, 1922, op. cit.
12. Arthur Walworth, "The Historical Significance of the House Diary," Yale University Press, 1996, pg. 6.
13. Walworth, pg. 7.
14. George Sylvester Viereck *The Strangest Friendship in His-*

Liveright, Inc., 1932), p. 28.

15. Walworth, pg. 2.

16. Seymour, p. 115.

17. Baker, op. cit., pg. 142.

18. G. Edward Griffin, *The Creature from Jekyll Island: A Second Look at the Federal Reserve* (Appleton, WI: American Opinion, 1994), 3-23.

19. House, *Liberty* magazine, January 7, 1933, as quoted in "Philip Dru: Fascist Prototype," J.B. Matthews, *American Mercury*, November 1954, 133-134.

20 Seymour, 160-161.

20. Bennett, John C. *Social Salvation: A Religious Approach to the Problems of Social Change* (New York: Charles Scribner's Sons, 1935), p. 165; as quoted in Alan Stang, *The Actor* (Boston: Western Islands, 1968), p. 80.

21. House, *Liberty*, September 14, 1935, as quoted in Matthews, op. cit., 140-141.

22. For a concise treatment of the Fascist origins of FDR's New Deal, see "FDR and Clinton: Goose-stepping to the Beat of the Same Drum" by William F. Jasper, *The New American,* April 5, 1993. Scholarly treatments of the same subject are found in Charlotte Twight, *Our Emerging Fascist Economy* (Arlington House, 1975); Leonard Piekoff, *The Ominous Parallels* (New York: Stein and Day, 1982); John T. Flynn, *As We Go Marching* (Garden City, N.Y.: Doubleday, Doran, 1944) and *The Roosevelt Myth* (New York, Devin-Adair, 1956).

23. Westbrook Pegler, "A Guide for Revolution," *Los Angeles Examiner*, September 13, 1954, 1-21.

24. Ibid.

25. Westbrook Pegler, "U.S. Fascism Spawned in 1912," *Los Angeles Examiner*, August 26, 1954, 1-25.

26. Pegler, op. cit.

27. Pegler, "A Guide for Revolution," op. cit.

28. Pegler, op. cit.

(Significant text of the title page for the
B.W. Huebsch 1919 edition)

PHILIP DRU: ADMINISTRATOR

A STORY OF TOMMORROW

1920–1935

"No war of classes, no hostility to existing wealth, no
wanton or unjust violation of the rights of property, but
a constant disposition to ameliorate the condition of the
classes least favored by fortune."

— MAZZINI.

This book is dedicated to the unhappy many who have lived and died lacking opportunity, because, in the starting, the world-wide social structure was wrongly begun.

Publisher's note:
The above dedication appeared in the 1919 edition.

CONTENTS

CONTENTS, Continued

CHAPTER I

Graduation Day

IN THE year 1920, the student and the statesman saw many indications that the social, financial and industrial troubles that had vexed the United States of America for so long a time were about to culminate in civil war.

Wealth had grown so strong, that the few were about to strangle the many, and among the great masses of the people, there was sullen and rebellious discontent.

The laborer in the cities, the producer on the farm, the merchant, the professional man and all save organized capital and its satellites, saw a gloomy and hopeless future.

With these conditions prevailing, the graduation exercises of the class of 1920 of the National Military Academy at West Point, held for many a foreboding promise of momentous changes, but the 12th of June found the usual gay scene at the great institution overlooking the Hudson. The President of the Republic, his Secretary of War and many other distinguished guests were there to do honor to the occasion, together with friends, relatives and admirers of the young men who were being sent out to the ultimate leadership of the Nation's Army. The scene had all the usual charm of West Point graduations, and the usual intoxicating atmosphere of military display.

There was among the young graduating soldiers one who seemed depressed and out of touch with the triumphant blare of militarism, for he alone of his fellow classmen had there no kith nor kin to bid him God-speed in his new career.

Standing apart under the broad shadow of an oak, he looked out over long stretches of forest and river, but what he saw was his home in distant Kentucky—the old farmhouse that the sun

1

and the rain and the lichens had softened into a mottled gray. He saw the gleaming brook that wound its way through the tangle of orchard and garden, and parted the distant blue-grass meadow.

He saw his aged mother sitting under the honeysuckle trellis, book in hand, but thinking, he knew, of him. And then there was the perfume of the flowers, the droning of the bees in the warm sweet air and the drowsy hound at his father's feet.

But this was not all the young man saw, for Philip Dru, in spite of his military training, was a close student of the affairs of his country, and he saw that which raised grave doubts in his mind as to the outcome of his career. He saw many of the civil institutions of his country debased by the power of wealth under the thin guise of the constitutional protection of property. He saw the Army which he had sworn to serve faithfully becoming prostituted by this same power, and used at times for purposes of intimidation and petty conquests where the interests of wealth were at stake. He saw the great city where luxury, dominant and defiant, existed largely by grace of exploitation—exploitation of men, women and children.

The young man's eyes had become bright and hard, when his day-dream was interrupted, and he was looking into the gray-blue eyes of Gloria Strawn—the one whose lot he had been comparing to that of her sisters in the city, in the mills, the sweatshops, the big stores, and the streets. He had met her for the first time a few hours before, when his friend and classmate, Jack Strawn, had presented him to his sister. No comrade knew Dru better than Strawn, and no one admired him so much. Therefore, Gloria, ever seeking a closer contact with life, had come to West Point eager to meet the lithe young Kentuckian, and to measure him by the other men of her acquaintance.

She was disappointed in his appearance, for she had fancied him almost god-like in both size and beauty, and she saw a man of medium height, slender but toughly knit, and with a strong, but homely face. When he smiled and spoke she forgot her disappointment, and her interest revived, for her sharp city sense caught the trail of a new experience.

To Philip Dru, whose thought of and experience with women was almost nothing, so engrossed had he been in his studies, military and economic, Gloria seemed little more than a child. And yet her frank glance of appraisal when he had been introduced to her, and her easy though somewhat languid conversation on the affairs of the commencement, perplexed and slightly annoyed him. He even felt some embarrassment in her presence.

Child though he knew her to be, he hesitated whether he should call her by her given name, and was taken aback when she smilingly thanked him for doing so, with the assurance that she was often bored with the eternal conventionality of people in her social circle.

Suddenly turning from the commonplaces of the day, Gloria looked directly at Philip, and with easy self-possession turned the conversation to himself.

"I am wondering, Mr. Dru, why you came to West Point and why it is you like the thought of being a soldier?" she asked. "An American soldier has to fight so seldom that I have heard that the insurance companies regard them as the best of risks, so what attraction, Mr. Dru, can a military career have for you?"

Never before had Philip been asked such a question, and it surprised him that it should come from this slip of a girl, but he answered her in the serious strain of his thoughts.

"As far back as I can remember," he said, "I have wanted to

be a soldier. I have no desire to destroy and kill, and yet there is within me the lust for action and battle. It is the primitive man in me, I suppose, but sobered and enlightened by civilization. I would do everything in my power to avert war and the suffering it entails. Fate, inclination, or what not has brought me here, and I hope my life may not be wasted, but that in God's own way, I may be a humble instrument for good. Oftentimes our inclinations lead us in certain directions, and it is only afterwards that it seems as if fate may from the first have so determined it."

The mischievous twinkle left the girl's eyes, and the languid tone of her voice changed to one a little more like sincerity.

"But suppose there is no war," she demanded, "suppose you go on living at barracks here and there, and with no broader outlook than such a life entails, will you be satisfied? Is that all you have in mind to do in the world?"

He looked at her more perplexed than ever. Such an observation of life, his life, seemed beyond her years, for he knew but little of the women of his own generation. He wondered, too, if she would understand if he told her all that was in his mind.

"Gloria, we are entering a new era. The past is no longer to be a guide to the future. A century and a half ago there arose in France a giant that had slumbered for untold centuries. He knew he had suffered grievous wrongs, but he did not know how to right them. He therefore struck out blindly and cruelly, and the innocent went down with the guilty. He was almost wholly ignorant for in the scheme of society as then constructed, the ruling few felt that he must be kept ignorant, otherwise they could not continue to hold him in bondage. For him the door of opportunity was closed, and he struggled from the cradle to the grave for the minimum of food and clothing necessary to keep breath within the body. His labor and his very life itself was subject to the greed, the passion and the caprice of his over-lord.

"So when he awoke he could only destroy. Unfortunately for him, there was not one of the governing class who was big enough and humane enough to lend a guiding and a friendly hand, so he was led by weak and selfish men who could only incite him to further wanton murder and demolition.

"But out of that revelry of blood there dawned upon mankind the hope of a more splendid day. The divinity of kings, the God-given right to rule, was shattered for all time. The giant at last knew his strength, and with head erect, and the light of freedom in his eyes, he dared to assert the liberty, equality and fraternity of man. Then throughout the Western world one stratum of society after another demanded and obtained the right to acquire wealth and to share in the government. Here and there one bolder and more forceful than the rest acquired great wealth and with it great power. Not satisfied with reasonable gain, they sought to multiply it beyond all bounds of need. They who had sprung from the people a short life span ago were now throttling individual effort and shackling the great movement for equal rights and equal opportunity."

Dru's voice became tense and vibrant, and he talked in quick sharp jerks.

"Nowhere in the world is wealth more defiant, and monopoly more insistent than in this mighty republic," he said, "and it is here that the next great battle for human emancipation will be fought and won. And from the blood and travail of an enlightened people, there will be born a spirit of love and brotherhood which will transform the world; and the Star of Bethlehem, seen but darkly for two thousand years, will shine again with a steady and effulgent glow."

CHAPTER II

The Vision of Philip Dru

LONG before Philip had finished speaking, Gloria saw that he had forgotten her presence. With glistening eyes and face aflame he had talked on and on with such compelling force that she beheld in him the prophet of a new day.

She sat very still for a while, and then she reached out to touch his sleeve.

"I think I understand how you feel now," she said in a tone different from any she had yet used. "I have been reared in a different atmosphere from you, and at home have heard only the other side, while at school they mostly evade the question. My father is one of the 'bold and forceful few' as perhaps you know, but he does not seem to me to want to harm anyone. He is kind to us, and charitable too, as that word is commonly used, and I am sure he has done much good with his money."

"I am sorry, Gloria, if I have hurt you by what I said," answered Dru.

"Oh! never mind, for I am sure you are right," answered the girl, but Philip continued—

"Your father, I think, is not to blame. It is the system that is a fault. His struggle and his environment from childhood have blinded him to the truth. To those with whom he has come in contact, it has been the dollar and not the man that counted. He has been schooled to think that capital can buy labor as it would machinery, the human equation not entering into it. He believes that it would be equivalent to confiscation for the State to say 'in regard to a corporation, labor, the State and capital are important in the order named.' Good man that he means to be, he

7

does not know, perhaps he can never know, that it is labor, labor of the mind and of the body, that creates, and not capital."

"You would have a hard time making Father see that," put in Gloria, with a smile.

"Yes!" continued Philip, "from the dawn of the world until now, it has been the strong against the weak. At the first, in the Stone Age, it was brute strength that counted and controlled. Then those that ruled had leisure to grow intellectually, and it gradually came about that the many, by long centuries of oppression, thought that the intellectual few had God-given powers to rule, and to exact tribute from them to the extent of commanding every ounce of exertion of which their bodies were capable. It was here, Gloria, that society began to form itself wrongly, and the result is the miserable travesty of today. Selfishness became the keynote, and to physical and mental strength was conceded everything that is desirable in life. Later, this mockery of justice, was partly recognized, and it was acknowledged to be wrong for the physically strong to despoil and destroy the physically weak. *Even so, the time is now measurably near when it will be just as reprehensible for the mentally strong to hold in subjection the mentally weak, and to force them to bear the grievous burdens which a misconceived civilization has imposed upon them.*"

Gloria was now thoroughly interested, but smilingly belied it by saying, "A history professor I had once lost his position for talking like that."

The young man barely recognized the interruption.

"The first gleam of hope came with the advent of Christ," he continued. "So warped and tangled had become the minds of men that the meaning of Christ's teaching failed utterly to reach human comprehension. They accepted him as a religious teacher only so far as their selfish desires led them. They were willing to deny other gods and admit one Creator of all things, but they split into fragments regarding the creeds and forms necessary to salvation. In the name of Christ they committed atrocities that would put to blush the most benighted savages. Their very excesses in cruelty finally caused a revolution in feeling, and there was evolved the Christian religion of to-day, a religion almost wholly selfish and concerned almost entirely in the betterment of life after death."

The girl regarded Philip for a second in silence, and then quietly asked, "For the betterment of whose life after death?"

"I was speaking of those who have carried on only the forms of religion. Wrapped in the sanctity of their own small circle, they feel that their tiny souls are safe, and that they are following the example and precepts of Christ.

"The full splendor of Christ's love, the grandeur of His life and doctrine is to them a thing unknown. The infinite love, the sweet humility, the gentle charity, the subordination of self that the Master came to give a cruel, selfish and ignorant world, mean but little more to us to-day than it did to those to whom He gave it."

"And you who have chosen a military career say this," said the girl as her brother joined the pair.

To Philip her comment came as something of a shock, for he was unprepared for these words spoken with such a depth of feeling.

Gloria and Philip Dru spent most of graduation day together. He did not want to intrude amongst the relatives and friends of his classmates, and he was eager to continue his acquaintance with Gloria. To the girl, this serious-minded youth who seemed so strangely out of tune with the blatant military fanfare, was a distinct novelty. At the final ball she almost ignored the gallantries of the young officers, in order that she might have opportunity to lead Dru on to further self-revelation.

The next day in the hurry of packing and departure he saw her only for an instant, but from her brother he learned that she planned to visit to the new Post on the Rio Grande near Eagle Pass where Jack Strawn and Philip were to be stationed after their vacation.

Philip spent his leave, before he went to the new Post, at his Kentucky home. He wanted to be with his father and mother, and he wanted to read and think, so he declined the many invitations to visit.

His father was a sturdy farmer of fine natural sense, and with him Philip never tired of talking when both had leisure.

Old William Dru had inherited nothing save a run-down, badly managed, heavily mortgaged farm that had been in the family for several generations. By hard work and strict economy, he had first built it up into a productive property and had then liquidated the indebtedness. So successful had he been that he was able to buy small farms for four of his sons, and give professional education to the other three. He had accumulated nothing, for he had given as fast as he had made, but his was a serene and contented old age because of it. What was the hoarding of money or land in comparison to the satisfaction of seeing each son happy in the possession of a home and family? The ancestral farm he intended for Philip, youngest and best beloved, soldier though he was to be.

All during that hot summer, Philip and his father discussed the ever-growing unrest of the country, and speculated when the crisis would come, and how it would end.

Finally, he left his home, and all the associations clustered around it, and turned his face towards imperial Texas, the field of his new endeavor.

He reached Fort Magruder at the close of an Autumn day.

He thought he had never known such dry sweet air. Just as the sun was sinking, he strolled to the bluff around which flowed the turbid waters of the Rio Grande, and looked across at the gray hills of old Mexico.

CHAPTER III

Lost in the Desert

AUTUMN drifted into winter, and then with the blossoms of an early spring, came Gloria.

The Fort was several miles from the station, and Jack and Philip were there to meet her. As they paced the little board platform, Jack was nervously happy over the thought of his sister's arrival, and talked of his plans for entertaining her. Philip on the other hand held himself well in reserve and gave no outward indication of the deep emotion which stirred within him. At last the train came and from one of the long string of Pullmans, Gloria alighted. She kissed her brother and greeted Philip cordially, and asked him in a tone of banter how he enjoyed army life. Dru smiled and said, "Much better, Gloria, than you predicted I would." The baggage was stored away in the buck-board, and Gloria got in front with Philip and they were off. It was early morning and the dew was still on the soft mesquite grass, and as the mustang ponies swiftly drew them over the prairie, it seemed to Gloria that she had awakened in fairyland.

At the crest of a hill, Philip held the horses for a moment, and Gloria caught her breath as she saw the valley below. It looked as if some translucent lake had mirrored the sky. It was the countless blossoms of the Texas blue-bonnet that lifted their slender stems towards the morning sun, and hid the earth.

Down into the valley they drove upon the most wonderfully woven carpet in all the world. Aladdin and his magic looms could never have woven a fabric such as this. A heavy, delicious perfume permeated the air, and with glistening eyes and parted lips, Gloria sat dumb in happy astonishment.

They dipped into the rocky bed of a wet weather stream, climbed out of the canyon and found themselves within the shadow of Fort Magruder.

Gloria soon saw that the social distractions of the place had little call for Philip. She learned, too, that he had already won the profound respect and liking of his brother officers. Jack spoke of him in terms even more superlative than ever. "He is a born leader of men," he declared, "and he knows more about engineering and tactics than the Colonel and all the rest of us put together." Hard student though he was, Gloria found him ever ready to devote himself to her, and their rides together over the boundless, flower studded prairies, were a never ending joy. "Isn't it beautiful—Isn't it wonderful," she would exclaim. And once she said, "But, Philip, happy as I am, I oftentimes think of the reeking poverty in the great cities, and wish, in some way, they could share this with me." Philip looked at her questioningly, but made no reply.

A visit that was meant for weeks transgressed upon the months, and still she lingered. One hot June morning found Gloria and Philip far in the hills on the Mexican side of the Rio Grande. They had started at dawn with the intention of breakfasting with the courtly old haciendado, who frequently visited at the Post.

After the ceremonious Mexican breakfast, Gloria wanted to see beyond the rim of the little world that enclosed the hacienda, so they rode to the end of the valley, tied their horses and climbed to the crest of the ridge. She was eager to go still further. They went down the hill on the other side, through a draw and into another valley beyond.

Soldier though he was, Philip was no plainsman, and in retracing their steps, they missed the draw. Philip knew that they were not going as they came, but with his months of experience in the hills, felt sure he could find his way back with less trouble by continuing as they were. The grass and the shrubs gradually disappeared as they walked, and soon he realized that they were on the edge of an alkali desert. Still he thought he could swing around into the valley from which they started, and they plunged steadily on, only to see in a few minutes that they were lost.

"What's the matter, Philip?" asked Gloria. "Are we lost?"

"I hope not, we only have to find that draw."

The girl said no more, but walked on side by side with the young soldier. Both pulled their hats far down over their eyes to shield them from the glare of the fierce rays of the sun, and did what they could to keep out the choking clouds of alkali dust that swirled around them at every step.

Philip, hardened by months of Southwestern service, stood the heat well, except that his eyes ached, but he saw that Gloria was giving out.

"Are you tired?" he asked.

"Yes, I am very tired," she answered, "but I can go on if you will let me rest a moment." Her voice was weak and uncertain and indicated approaching collapse. And then she said more faintly, "I am afraid, Philip, we are hopelessly lost."

"Do not be frightened, Gloria, we will soon be out of this if you will let me carry you."

Just then, the girl staggered and would have fallen had he not caught her.

He was familiar with heat prostration, and saw that her condition was not serious, but he knew he must carry her, for to lay her in the blazing sun would be fatal.

His eyes, already overworked by long hours of study, were swollen and bloodshot. Sharp pains shot through his head. To stop he feared would be to court death, so taking Gloria in his

15

arms, he staggered on.

In that vast world of alkali and adobe there was no living thing but these two. No air was astir, and a pitiless sun beat upon them unmercifully.

Philip's lips were cracked, his tongue was swollen, and the burning dust almost choked him. He began to see less clearly, and visions of things he knew to be unreal came to him. With Spartan courage and indomitable will, he never faltered, but went on. Mirages came and went, and he could not know whether he saw true or not. Then here and there he thought he began to see tufts of curly mesquite grass, and in the distance surely there were cacti. He knew that if he could hold out a little longer, he could lay his burden in some sort of shade.

With halting steps, with eyes inflamed and strength all but gone, he finally laid Gloria in the shadow of a giant prickly pear bush, and fell beside her. He fumbled for his knife and clumsily scraped the needles from a leaf of the cactus and sliced it in two. The heavy sticky liquid ran over his hand as he placed the cut side of the leaf to Gloria's lips. The juice of the plant together with the shade, partially revived her. Philip, too, sucked the leaf until his parched tongue and throat became a little more pliable.

"What happened?" demanded Gloria. "Oh! yes, now I remember. I am sorry I gave out, Philip. I am not acclimated yet. What time is it?"

After pillowing her head more comfortably upon his riding coat, Philip looked at his watch.

"I—I can't just make it out, Gloria," he said. "My eyes seem blurred. This awful glare seems to have affected them. They'll be all right in a little while."

Gloria looked at the dial and found that the hands pointed to four o'clock. They had been lost for six hours, but after their experiences, it seemed more like as many days. They rested a little while longer talking but little.

"You carried me," said Gloria once. "I'm ashamed of myself for letting the heat get the best of me. You shouldn't have carried me, Philip, but you know I understand and appreciate. How are your eyes now?"

"Oh, they'll be all right," he reiterated, but when he took his hand from them to look at her, and the light beat upon the inflamed lids, he winced.

After eating some of the fruit of the prickly pear, which they found too hot and sweet to be palatable, Philip suggested at half after five that they should move on. They arose, and the young officer started to lead the way, peeping from beneath his hand. First he stumbled over a mesquite bush directly in his path, and next he collided with a giant cactus standing full in front of him.

"It's no use, Gloria," he said at last. "I can't see the way. You must lead."

"All right, Philip, I will do the best I can."

For answer, he merely took her hand, and together they started to retrace their steps. Over the trackless waste of alkali and sagebrush they trudged. They spoke but little but when they did, their husky, dust-parched voices made a mockery of their hopeful words.

Though the horizon seemed bounded by a low range of hills, the girl instinctively turned her steps westward, and entered a draw. She rounded one of the hills, and just as the sun was sinking, came upon the valley in which their horses were peacefully grazing.

They mounted and followed the dim trail along which they had ridden that morning, reaching the hacienda about dark. With many shakings of the hand, voluble protestations of joy at their delivery from the desert, and callings on God to witness that the girl had performed a miracle, the haciendado gave them food and cooling drinks, and with gentle insistence, had his servants, wife and daughters show them to their rooms. A poultice of Mexican herbs was laid across Philip's eyes, but exhausted as he was he could not sleep because of the pain they caused him.

In the morning, Gloria was almost her usual self, but Philip could see but faintly. As early as was possible they started for Fort Magruder. His eyes were bandaged, and Gloria held the bridle of his horse and led him along the dusty trail. A vaquero from the ranch went with them to show the way.

Then came days of anxiety, for the surgeon at the Post saw serious trouble ahead for Philip. He would make no definite statement, but admitted that the brilliant young officer's eyesight was seriously menaced.

Gloria read to him and wrote for him, and in many ways was his hands and eyes. He in turn talked to her of the things that filled his mind. The betterment of man was an ever-present theme with them. It pleased him to trace for her the world's history from its early beginning when all was misty tradition, down through the uncertain centuries of early civilization to the present time.

He talked with her of the untrustworthiness of the so-called history of to-day, although we had every facility for recording facts, and he pointed out how utterly unreliable it was when tradition was the only means of transmission. Mediocrity, he felt sure, had oftentimes been exalted into genius, and brilliant and patriotic exclamations attributed to great men, were never uttered by them, neither was it easy he thought, to get a true historic picture of the human intellectual giant. As a rule they were quite human, but people insisted upon idealizing them, consequently they became not themselves but what the popular mind wanted them to be.

He also dwelt on the part the demagogue and the incompetents play in retarding the advancement of the human race. Some leaders were honest, some were wise and some were selfish, but it was seldom that the people would be led by wise, honest and unselfish men.

"There is always the demagogue to poison the mind of the people against such a man," he said, "and it is easily done because wisdom means moderation and honesty means truth. To be moderate and to tell the truth at all times and about all matters seldom pleases the masses."

Many a long day was spent thus in purely impersonal discussions of affairs, and though he himself did not realize it, Gloria saw that Philip was ever at his best when viewing the large questions of State, rather than the narrower ones within the scope of the military power.

The weeks passed swiftly, for the girl knew well how to ease the young Officer's chafing at uncertainty and inaction. At times, as they droned away the long hot summer afternoons under the heavily leafed fig trees in the little garden of the Strawn bungalow, he would become impatient at his enforced idleness. Finally one day, after making a pitiful attempt to read, Philip broke out, "I have been patient under this as long as I can. The restraint is too much. Something must be done."

Somewhat to his surprise, Gloria did not try to take his mind off the situation this time, but suggested asking the surgeon for a definite report on his condition.

The interview with the surgeon was unsatisfactory, but his report to his superior officers bore fruit, for in a short time Philip was told that he should apply for an indefinite leave of absence, as it would be months, perhaps years, before his eyes would allow him to carry on his duties.

He seemed dazed at the news, and for a long time would not talk of it even with Gloria. After a long silence one afternoon she softly asked, "What are you going to do, Philip?"

Jack Strawn, who was sitting near by, broke out — "Do! why there's no question about what he is going to do. Once an Army man always an Army man. He's going to live on the best the U. S. A. provides until his eyes are right. In the meantime Philip is going to take indefinite sick leave."

The girl only smiled at her brother's military point of view, and asked another question. "How will you occupy your time, Philip?"

Philip sat as if he had not heard them.

"Occupy his time!" exclaimed Jack, "getting well of course. Without having to obey orders or do anything but draw his checks, he can have the time of his life, there will be nothing to worry about."

"That's just it," slowly said Philip. "No work, nothing to think about."

"Exactly," said Gloria.

"What are you driving at, Sister. You talk as if it was something to be deplored. I call it a lark. Cheer the fellow up a bit, can't you?"

"No, never mind," replied Philip. "There's nothing to cheer me up about. The question is simply this: Can I stand a period of several years' enforced inactivity as a mere pensioner?"

"Yes!" quickly said Gloria, "as a pensioner, and then, if all goes well, you return to this."

"What do you mean, Gloria? Don't you like Army Post life?" asked Jack.

"I like it as well as you do, Jack. You just haven't come to realize that Philip is cut out for a bigger sphere than — that."

She pointed out across the parade ground where a drill was going on. "You know as well as I do that this is not the age for a military career."

Jack was so disgusted with this, that with an exclamation of impatience, he abruptly strode off to the parade ground.

"You are right, Gloria," said Philip. "I cannot live on a pension indefinitely. I cannot bring myself to believe that it is honest to become a mendicant upon the bounty of the country. If I had been injured in the performance of duty, I would have no scruples in accepting support during an enforced idleness, but this disability arose from no fault of the Government, and the thought of accepting aid under such circumstances is too repugnant."

"Of course," said Gloria.

"The Government means no more to me than an individual," continued Philip, "and it is to be as fairly dealt with. I never could understand how men with self-respect could accept undeserving pensions from the Nation. To do so is not alone dishonest, but is unfair to those who need help and have a righteous claim to support. If the unworthy were refused, the deserving would be able to obtain that to which they are entitled."

Their talk went on thus for hours, the girl ever trying more particularly to make him see a military career as she did, and he more concerned with the ethical side of the situation.

"Do not worry over it, Philip," cried Gloria, "I feel sure that your place is in the larger world of affairs, and you will some day be glad that this misfortune came to you, and that you were forced to go into another field of endeavor.

"With my ignorance and idle curiosity, I led you on and on, over first one hill and then another, until you lost your way in that awful desert over there, but yet perhaps there was a destiny in that. When I was leading you out of the desert, a blind man, it may be that I was leading you out of the barrenness of military life, into the fruitful field of labor for humanity."

After a long silence, Philip Dru arose and took Gloria's hand.

"Yes! I will resign. You have already reconciled me to my fate."

CHAPTER IV

The Supremacy of Mind

OFFICERS and friends urged Philip to reconsider his determination of resigning, but once decided, he could not be swerved from his purpose. Gloria persuaded him to go to New York with her in order to consult one of the leading oculists, and arrangements were made immediately.

On the last day but one, as they sat under their favorite fig tree, they talked much of Philip's future. Gloria had also been reading aloud Sir Oliver Lodge's "Science and Immortality," and closing the book upon the final chapter, asked Philip what he thought of it.

"Although the book was written many years ago, even then the truth had begun to dawn upon the poets, seers and scientific dreamers. The dominion of mind, but faintly seen at that time, but more clearly now, will finally come into full vision. The materialists under the leadership of Darwin, Huxley and Wallace, went far in the right direction, but in trying to go to the very fountainhead of life, they came to a door which they could not open and which no materialistic key will ever open."

"So, Mr. Preacher, you're at it again," laughed Gloria. "You belong to the pulpit of real life, not the Army. Go on, I am interested."

"Well," went on Dru, "then came a reaction, and the best thought of the scientific world swung back to the theory of mind or spirit, and the truth began to unfold itself. Now, man is at last about to enter into that splendid kingdom, the promise of which Christ gave us when he said, 'My Father and I are one,' and again, 'When you have seen me you have seen the Father.' He was but telling them that all life was a part of the

23

One Life — individualized, but yet of and a part of the whole.

"We are just learning our power and dominion over ourselves. When in the future children are trained from infancy that they can measurably conquer their troubles by the force of mind, a new era will have come to man."

"There," said Gloria, with an earnestness that Philip had rarely heard in her, "is perhaps the source of the true redemption of the world."

She checked herself quickly, "But you were preaching to me, not I to you. Go on."

"No, but I want to hear what you were going to say."

"You see I am greatly interested in this movement which is seeking to find how far mind controls matter, and to what extent our lives are spiritual rather than material," she answered, "but it's hard to talk about it to most people, so I have kept it to myself. Go on, Philip, I will not interrupt again."

"When fear, hate, greed and the purely material conception of Life passes out," said Philip, "as it some day may, and only wholesome thoughts will have a place in human minds, mental ills will take flight along with most of our bodily ills, and the miracle of the world's redemption will have been largely wrought."

"Mental ills will take flight along with bodily ills. We should be trained, too, not to dwell upon anticipated troubles, but to use our minds and bodies in an earnest, honest endeavor to avert threatened disaster. We should not brood over possible failure, for in the great realm of the supremacy of mind or spirit the thought of failure should not enter."

"Yes, I know, Philip."

"Fear, causes perhaps more unhappiness than any one thing that we have let take possession of us. Some are never free from it. They awake in the morning with a vague, indefinite sense of it, and at night a foreboding of disaster hands over the to-morrow. Life would have for us a different meaning if we would resolve, and keep the resolution, to do the best we could under all conditions, and never fear the result. Then, too, we should be trained not to have such an unreasonable fear of death. The Eastern peoples are far wiser in this respect than we. They have learned to look upon death as a happy transition to something better. And they are right, for that is the true philosophy of it. At the very worst, can it mean more than a long and dreamless sleep? Does not the soul either go back to the one source from which it sprung, and become a part of the whole, or does it not throw off its material environment and continue with individual consciousness to work out its final destiny?

"If that be true, there is no death as we have conceived it. It would mean to us merely the beginning of a more splendid day, and we should be taught that every emotion, every effort here that is unselfish and soul uplifting, will better fit us for that spiritual existence that is to come."

CHAPTER V

The Tragedy of the Turners

THE trip north from Fort Magruder was a most trying experience for Philip Dru, for although he had as traveling companions Gloria and Jack Strawn, who was taking a leave of absence, the young Kentuckian felt his departure from Texas and the Army as a portentous turning point in his career. In spite of Gloria's philosophy, and in spite of Jack's reassurances, Philip was assailed by doubts as to the ultimate improvement of his eyesight, and at the same time with the feeling that perhaps after all, he was playing the part of a deserter.

"It's all nonsense to feel cut up over it, you know, Philip," insisted Jack. "You can take my word for it that you have the wrong idea in wanting to quit when you can be taken care of by the Government. You have every right to it."

"No, Jack, I have no right to it," answered Dru, "but certain as I am that I am doing the only thing I could do, under the circumstances, it's a hard wrench to leave the Army, even though I had come to think that I can find my place in the world out of the service."

The depression was not shaken off until after they had reached New York, and Philip had been told by the great specialist that his eyesight probably never again would pass the Army tests. Once convinced that an Army career was impossible, he resigned, and began to reconstruct his life with new hope and with a new enthusiasm. While he was ordered to give his eyes complete rest for at least six months and remain a part of every day in a darkened room, he was promised that after several months, he probably would be able to read and write a little.

As he had no relatives in New York, Philip, after some hesitation, accepted Jack Strawn's insistent invitation to visit him for a time, at least. Through the long days and weeks that followed, the former young officer and Gloria were thrown much together.

One afternoon as they were sitting in a park, a pallid child of ten asked to "shine" their shoes. In sympathy they allowed him to do it. The little fellow had a gaunt and hungry look and his movements were very sluggish. He said his name was Peter Turner and he gave some squalid east side tenement district as his home. He said that his father was dead, his mother was bedridden, and he, the oldest of three children, was the only support of the family. He got up at five and prepared their simple meal, and did what he could towards making his mother comfortable for the day. By six he left the one room that sheltered them, and walked more than two miles to where he now was. Midday meal he had none, and in the late afternoon he walked home and arranged their supper of bread, potatoes, or whatever else he considered he could afford to buy. Philip questioned him as to his earnings and was told that they varied with the weather and other conditions, the maximum had been a dollar and fifteen cents for one day, the minimum twenty cents. The average seemed around fifty cents, and this was to shelter, clothe and feed a family of four.

Already Gloria's eyes were dimmed with tears. Philip asked if they might go home with him then. The child consented and led the way.

They had not gone far, when Philip, noticing how frail Peter was, hailed a car, and they rode to Grand Street, changed there and went east. Midway between the Bowery and the river, they got out and walked south for a few blocks, turned into a side street that was hardly more than an alley, and came to the tenement where Peter lived.

It had been a hot day even in the wide, clean portions of the city. Here the heat was almost unbearable, and the stench, incident to a congested population, made matters worse.

Ragged and dirty children were playing in the street. Lack of food and pure air, together with unsanitary surroundings, had set its mark upon them. The deathly pallor that was in Peter's face was characteristic of most of the faces around them.

The visitors climbed four flights of stairs, and went down a long, dark, narrow hall reeking with disagreeable odors, and finally entered ten-year-old Peter Turner's "home."

"What a travesty on the word 'home,'" murmured Dru, as he saw for the first time the interior of an East Side tenement. Mrs. Turner lay propped in bed, a ghost of what was once a comely woman. She was barely thirty, yet poverty, disease and the city had drawn their cruel lines across her face. Gloria went to her bedside and gently pressed the fragile hand. She dared not trust herself to speak. And this, she thought, is within the shadow of my home, and I never knew. "Oh, God," she silently prayed, "forgive us for our neglect of such as these."

Gloria and Philip did all that was possible for the Turners, but their helping hands came too late to do more than to give the mother a measure of peace during the last days of her life. The promise of help for the children lifted a heavy load from her heart. Poor stricken soul, Zelda Turner deserved a better fate. When she married Len Turner, life seemed full of joy. He was employed in the office of a large manufacturing concern, at what seemed to them a munificent salary, seventy-five dollars a month.

Those were happy days. How they saved and planned for the future! The castle that they built in Spain was a little home on a small farm near a city large enough to be a profitable market for their produce. Some place where the children could get fresh air, wholesome food and a place in which to grow up. Two thousand dollars saved, would, they thought, be enough to make the start. With this, a farm costing four thousand dollars could be bought by mortgaging it for half. Twenty-five dollars a month saved for six years, would, with interest, bring them to their goal.

Already more than half the sum was theirs. Then came disaster. One Sunday they were out for their usual walk. It had been sleeting and the pavements here and there were still icy. In front of them some children were playing, and a little girl of eight darted into the street to avoid being caught by a companion. She slipped and fell. A heavy motor was almost upon her, when Len rushed to snatch her from the on-rushing car. He caught the child, but slipped himself, succeeding however in pushing her beyond danger before the cruel wheels crushed out his life. The dreary days and nights that followed need not be recited here. The cost of the funeral and other expenses incident thereto bit deep into their savings, therefore as soon as she could pull herself together, Mrs. Turner sought employment and got it in a large dressmaking establishment at the inadequate wage of seven dollars a week. She was skillful with her needle but had no aptitude for design, therefore she was ever to be among the plodders. One night in the busy season of overwork before the Christmas holidays, she started to walk the ten blocks to her little home, for car-fare was a tax beyond her purse, and losing her weary footing, she fell heavily to the ground. By the aid of a kindly policeman she was able to reach home, in great suffering, only to faint when she finally reached her room. Peter, who was then about seven years old, was badly frightened. He ran for their next door neighbor, a kindly

German woman. She lifted Zelda into bed and sent for a physician, and although he could find no other injury than a badly bruised spine, she never left her bed until she was borne to her grave.

The pitiful little sum that was saved soon went, and Peter with his blacking box became the sole support of the family.

When they had buried Zelda, and Gloria was kneeling by her grave softly weeping, Philip touched her shoulder and said, "Let us go, she needs us no longer, but there are those who do. This experience has been my lesson, and from now it is my purpose to consecrate my life towards the betterment of such as these. Our thoughts, our habits, our morals, our civilization itself is wrong, else it would not be possible for just this sort of suffering to exist."

"But you will let me help you, Philip?" said Gloria.

"It will mean much to me, Gloria, if you will. In this instance Len Turner died a hero's death, and when Mrs. Turner became incapacitated, society, the state, call it what you will, should have stepped in and thrown its protecting arms around her. It was never intended that she should lie there day after day, month after month, suffering, starving, and in an agony of soul for her children's future. She had the right to expect succor from the rich and the strong."

"Yes," said Gloria, "I have heard successful men and women say that they cannot help the poor, that if you gave them all you had, they would soon be poor again, and that your giving would never cease."

"I know," Philip replied, "that is ever the cry of the selfish. They believe that they merit all the blessings of health, distinction and wealth that may come to them, and they condemn their less fortunate brother as one deserving his fate. The poor, the weak and the impractical did not themselves bring about their condition. Who knows how large a part the mystery of birth and heredity play in one's life and what environment and opportunity, or lack of it, means to us? Health, ability, energy, favorable environment and opportunity are the ingredients of success. Success is graduated by the lack of one or all of these. If the powerful use their strength merely to further their own selfish desires, in what way save in degree do they differ from the lower animals of creation? And how can man under such a moral code justify his dominion over land and sea?

"Until recently this question has never squarely faced the human race, but it does face it now and to its glory and honor it is going to be answered right. The strong will help the weak, the rich will share with the poor, and it will not be called charity, but it will be known as justice. And the man or woman who fails to do his duty, not as he sees it, but as society at large sees it, will be held up to the contempt of mankind. A generation or two ago, Gloria, this mad unreasoning scramble for wealth began. Men have fought, struggled and died, lured by the gleam of gold, and to what end? The so-called fortunate few that succeed in obtaining it, use it in divers ways. To some, lavish expenditure and display pleases their swollen vanity. Others, more serious minded, gratify their selfishness by giving largess to schools of learning and research, and to the advancement of the sciences and arts. But here and there was found a man gifted beyond his fellows, one with vision clear enough to distinguish things worth while. And these, scorning to acquire either wealth or power, labored diligently in their separate fields of endeavor. One such became a great educator, the greatest of his day and generation, and by his long life of rectitude set an example to the youth of America that has done more good than all the gold that all the millionaires have given for educational purposes. Another brought to success a prodigious physical undertaking. For no further reason than that he might serve his country where best he could, he went into a fever-laden land and dug a mighty ditch, bringing together two great oceans and changing the commerce of the world."

CHAPTER VI

The Prophet of a New Day

PHILIP and Mr. Strawn oftentimes discussed the mental and moral upheaval that was now generally in evidence.

"What is to be the outcome, Philip?" said Mr. Strawn. "I know that things are not as they should be, but how can there be a more even distribution of wealth without lessening the efficiency of the strong, able and energetic men and without making mendicants of the indolent and improvident? If we had pure socialism, we could never get the highest endeavor out of anyone, for it would seem not worth while to do more than the average. The race would then go backward instead of lifting itself higher by the insistent desire to excel and to reap the rich reward that comes with success."

"In the past, Mr. Strawn, your contention would be unanswerable, but the moral tone and thought of the world is changing. You take it for granted that man must have in sight some material reward in order to bring forth the best there is within him. I believe that mankind is awakening to the fact that material compensation is far less to be desired than spiritual compensation. This feeling will grow, it is growing, and when it comes to full fruition, the world will find but little difficulty in attaining a certain measure of altruism. I agree with you that this much-to-be desired state of society cannot be altogether reached by laws, however drastic. Socialism as dreamed of by Karl Marx cannot be entirely brought about by a comprehensive system of state ownership and by the leveling of wealth. If that were done without a spiritual leavening, the result would be largely as you suggest."

And so the discussion ran, Strawn the embodiment of the old

order of thought and habit, and Philip the apostle of the new. And Gloria listened and felt that in Philip a new force had arisen. She likened him to a young eagle who, soaring high above a slumbering world, sees first the gleaming rays of that onrushing sun that is soon to make another day.

CHAPTER VII

The Winning of a Medal

IT HAD become the practice of the War Department to present to the army every five years a comprehensive military problem involving an imaginary attack upon this country by a powerful foreign foe, and the proper line of defense. The competition was open to both officers and men. A medal was given to the successful contestant, and much distinction came with it.

There had been as yet but one contest; five years before the medal had been won by a Major General who by wide acclaim was considered the greatest military authority in the Army. That he should win seemed to accord with the fitness of things, and it was thought that he would again be successful.

The problem had been given to the Army on the first of November, and six months were allowed to study it and hand in a written dissertation thereon. It was arranged that the general military staff that considered the papers should not know the names of the contestants.

Philip had worked upon the matter assiduously while he was at Fort Magruder, and had sent in his paper early in March. Great was his surprise upon receiving a telegram from the Secretary of War announcing that he had won the medal. For a few days he was a national sensation. The distinction of the first winner, who was again a contestant, and Philip's youth and obscurity, made such a striking contrast that the whole situation appealed enormously to the imagination of the people. Then, too, the problem was one of unusual interest, and it, as well as Philip's masterly treatment of it, was published far and wide.

The Nation was clearly treating itself to a sensation, and

upon Philip were focused the eyes of all. From now he was a marked man. The President, stirred by the wishes of a large part of the people, expressed by them in divers ways, offered him reinstatement in the Army with the rank of Major, and indicated, through the Secretary of War, that he would be assigned as Secretary to the General Staff. It was a gracious thing to do, even though it was prompted by that political instinct for which the President had become justly famous.

In an appreciative note of thanks, Philip declined. Again he became the talk of the hour. Poor, and until now obscure, it was assumed that he would gladly seize such an opportunity for a brilliant career within his profession. His friends were amazed and urged him to reconsider the matter, but his determination was fixed.

Only Gloria understood and approved.

"Philip," said Mr. Strawn, "do not turn this offer down lightly. Such an opportunity seldom comes twice in any man's life."

"I am deeply impressed with the truth of what you say, Mr. Strawn, and I am not putting aside a military career without much regret. However, I am now committed to a life work of a different character, one in which glory and success as the world knows it can never enter, but which appeals to every instinct that I possess. I have turned my face in the one direction, and come what may, I shall never change."

"I am afraid, Philip, that in the enthusiasm of youth and inexperience you are doing a foolish thing, one that will bring you many hours of bitter regret. This is the parting of the ways with you. Take the advice of one who loves you well and turn into the road leading to honor and success. The path which you are about to choose is obscure and difficult, and none may say just where it leads."

"What you say is true, Mr. Strawn, only we are measuring results by different standards. If I could journey your road with a blythe heart, free from regret, when glory and honor came, I should revel in it and die, perhaps, happy and contented. But constituted as I am, when I began to travel along that road, from its dust there would arise to haunt me the ghosts of those of my fellowmen who had lived and died without opportunity. The cold and hungry, the sick and suffering poor, would seem to cry to me that I had abandoned them in order that I might achieve distinction and success, and there would be for me no peace."

And here Gloria touched his hand with hers, that he might know her thoughts and sympathy were at one with his.

Philip was human enough to feel a glow of satisfaction at having achieved so much reputation. A large part of it, he felt, was undeserved and rather hysterical, but that he had been able to do a big thing made him surer of his ground in his new field of endeavor. He believed, too, that it would aid him largely in obtaining the confidence of those with whom he expected to work and of those he expected to work for.

CHAPTER VIII

The Story of the Levinskys

As SOON as public attention was brought to Philip in such a generous way, he received many offers to write for the press and magazines, and also to lecture.

He did not wish to draw upon his father's slender resources, and yet he must needs do something to meet his living expenses, for during the months of his inactivity, he had drawn largely upon the small sum which he had saved from his salary.

The Strawns were insistent that he should continue to make their home his own, but this he was unwilling to do. So he rented an inexpensive room over a small hardware store in the East Side tenement district. He thought of getting in one of the big, evil-smelling tenement houses so that he might live as those he came to help lived, but he abandoned this because he feared he might become too absorbed in those immediately around him.

What he wanted was a broader view. His purpose was not so much to give individual help as to formulate some general plan and to work upon those lines.

And yet he wished an intimate view of the things he meant to devote his life to bettering. So the clean little room over the quiet hardware store seemed to suit his wants.

The thin, sharp-featured Jew and his fat, homely wife who kept it had lived in that neighborhood for many years, and Philip found them a mine of useful information regarding the things he wished to know.

The building was narrow and but three stories high, and his landlord occupied all of the second story save the one room which was let to Philip.

He arranged with Mrs. Levinsky to have his breakfast with them. He soon learned to like the Jew and his wife. While they were kind-hearted and sympathetic, they seldom permitted their sympathy to encroach upon their purse, but this Philip knew was a matter of environment and early influence. He drew from them one day the story of their lives, and it ran like this:

Ben Levinsky's forebears had long lived in Warsaw. From father to son, from one generation to another, they had handed down a bookshop, which included bookbinding in a small way. They were self-educated and widely read. Their customers were largely among the gentiles and for a long time the anti-semitic waves passed over them, leaving them untouched. They were law-abiding, inoffensive, peaceable citizens, and had been for generations.

One bleak December day, at a market place in Warsaw, a young Jew, baited beyond endurance, struck out madly at his aggressors, and in the general mêlée that followed, the son of a high official was killed. No one knew how he became involved in the brawl, for he was a sober, high-minded youngster, and very popular. Just how he was killed and by whom was never known. But the Jew had struck the first blow and that was all sufficient for the blood of hate to surge in the eyes of the race-mad mob.

Then began a blind, unreasoning massacre. It all happened within an hour. It was as if after nightfall a tornado had come out of the west, and without warning had torn and twisted itself thru the city, leaving ruin and death in its wake. No Jew that could be found was spared. Saul Levinsky was sitting in his shop looking over some books that had just come from the binder. He heard shots in the distance and the dull, angry roar of the hoarse-voiced mob. He closed his door and bolted it, and went up the little stairs leading to his family quarters. His wife and six-year-old daughter were there. Ben, a boy of ten, had gone to a nobleman's home to deliver some books, and had not returned.

Levinsky expected the mob to pass his place and leave it unmolested. It stopped, hesitated and then rammed in the door. It was all over in a moment. Father, mother and child lay dead and torn almost limb from limb. The rooms were wrecked, and the mob moved on.

The tempest passed as quickly as it came, and when little Ben reached his home, the street was as silent as the grave.

With quivering lip and uncertain feet he picked his way from room to room until he came to what was once his father, mother and baby sister, and then he swooned away. When he awoke he was shivering with cold. For a moment he did not realize what had happened, then with a heartbreaking cry he fled the place, nor did he stop until he was a league away.

He crept under the sheltering eaves of a half-burned house, and cold and miserable he sobbed himself to sleep. In the morning an itinerant tinker came by and touched by the child's distress, drew from him his unhappy story. He was a lonely old man, and offered to take Ben with him, an offer which was gladly accepted.

We will not chronicle the wanderings of these two in pursuit of food and shelter, for it would take too long to tell in sequence how they finally reached America, of the tinker's death, and of the evolution of the tinker's pack to the well ordered hardware shop over which Philip lived.

CHAPTER IX

Philip Begins a New Career

AFTER sifting the offers made him, Philip finally accepted two, one from a large New York daily that syndicated throughout the country, and one from a widely read magazine, to contribute a series of twelve articles. Both the newspaper and the magazine wished to dictate the subject matter about which he was to write, but he insisted upon the widest latitude. The sum paid, and to be paid, seemed to him out of proportion to the service rendered, but he failed to take into account the value of the advertising to those who had secured the use of his pen.

He accepted the offers not alone because he must needs do something for a livelihood, but largely for the good he thought he might do the cause to which he was enlisted. He determined to write upon social subjects only, though he knew that this would be a disappointment to his publishers. He wanted to write an article or two before he began his permanent work, for if he wrote successfully, he thought it would add to his influence. So he began immediately, and finished his first contribution to the syndicate newspapers in time for them to use it the following Sunday.

He told in a simple way, the story of the Turners. In conclusion he said the rich and the well-to-do were as a rule charitable enough when distress came to their doors, but the trouble was that they were unwilling to seek it out. They knew that it existed but they wanted to come in touch with it as little as possible.

They smothered their consciences with the thought that there were organized societies and other mediums through which all poverty was reached, and to these they gave. They knew that this was not literally true, but it served to make them think less badly of themselves.

In a direct and forceful manner, he pointed out that our civilization was fundamentally wrong inasmuch as among other things, it restricted efficiency; that if society were properly organized, there would be none who were not sufficiently clothed and fed; that the laws, habits and ethical training in vogue were alike responsible for the inequalities in opportunity and the consequent wide difference between the few and the many; that the result of such conditions was to render inefficient a large part of the population, the percentage differing in each country in the ratio that education and enlightened and unselfish laws bore to ignorance, bigotry and selfish laws. But little progress, he said, had been made in the early centuries for the reason that opportunity had been confined to a few, and it was only recently that any considerable part of the world's population had been in a position to become efficient; and mark the result. Therefore, he argued, as an economical proposition, divorced from the realm of ethics, the far-sighted statesmen of to-morrow, if not of to-day, will labor to the end that every child born of woman may have an opportunity to accomplish that for which it is best fitted. Their bodies will be properly clothed and fed at the minimum amount of exertion, so that life may mean something more than a mere struggle for existence. Humanity as a whole will then be able to do its share towards the conquest of the complex forces of nature, and there will be brought about an intellectual and spiritual quickening that will make our civilization of to-day seem as crude, as selfish and illogical as that of the dark ages seem now to us.

Philip's article was widely read and was the subject of much comment, favorable and otherwise. There were the ever-ready few, who want to re-make the world in a day, that objected to its moderation, and there were his more numerous critics who hold that to those that have, more should be given. These considered his doctrine dangerous to the general welfare, meaning their own welfare. But upon the greater number it made a profound impression, and it awakened many a sleeping conscience as was shown by the hundreds of letters which he received from all parts of the country. All this was a tremendous encouragement to the young social worker, for the letters he received showed him that he had a definite public to address, whom he might lead if he could keep his medium for a time at least. Naturally, the publishers of the newspaper and magazine for which he wrote understood this, but they also understood that it was usually possible to control intractable writers after they had acquired a taste for publicity, and their attitude was for the time being one of general enthusiasm and liberality tempered by such trivial attempts at control as had already been made.

No sooner had he seen the first story in print than he began formulating his ideas for a second. This, he planned, would be a companion piece to that of the Turners which was typical of the native American family driven to the East Side by the inevitable workings of the social order, and would take up the problem of the foreigner immigrating to this country, and its effect upon our national life. In this second article he incorporated the story of the Levinskys as being fairly representative of the problem he wished to treat.

In preparing these articles, Philip had used his eyes for the first time in such work, and he was pleased to find no harm came of it. The oculist still cautioned moderation, but otherwise dismissed him as fully recovered.

CHAPTER X

Gloria Decides to Proselyte the Rich

WHILE Philip was establishing himself in New York, as a social worker and writer, Gloria was spending more and more of her time in settlement work, in spite of the opposition of her family. Naturally, their work brought them much into each other's society and drew them even closer together than in Philip's dark days when Gloria was trying to aid him in the readjustment of his life. They were to all appearances simply comrades in complete understanding, working together for a common cause.

However, Strawn's opposition to Gloria's settlement work was not all impersonal, for he made no secret of his worry over Gloria's evident admiration for Dru. Strawn saw in Philip a masterly man with a prodigious intellect, bent upon accomplishing a revolutionary adjustment of society, and he knew that nothing would deter him from his purpose. The magnitude of the task and the uncertainties of success made him fear that Gloria might become one of the many unhappy women who suffer martyrdom through the greatness of their love.

Gloria's mother felt the same way about her daughter's companion in settlement work. Mrs. Strawn was a placid, colorless woman, content to go the conventional way, without definite purpose, further than to avoid the rougher places in life.

She was convinced that men were placed here for the sole purpose of shielding and caring for women, and she had a contempt for any man who refused or was unable to do so.

Gloria's extreme advanced views of life alarmed her and seemed unnatural. She protested as strongly as she could, without upsetting her equanimity, for to go beyond that she felt was

49

unladylike and bad for both nerves and digestion. It was a grief for her to see Gloria actually working with anyone, much less Philip, whose theories were quite upsetting, and who, after all, was beyond the pale of their social sphere and was impossible as a son-in-law.

Consequently, Philip was not surprised when one day in the fall, he received a disconsolate note from Gloria who was spending a few weeks with her parents at their camp in the hills beyond Tuxedo, saying that her father had flatly refused to allow her to take a regular position with one of the New York settlements, which would require her living on the East Side instead of at home. The note concluded:

"Now, Philip, do come up for Sunday and let's talk it over, for I am sadly at variance with my family, and I need your assistance and advice.

"Yours very sincere,
"GLORIA."

The letter left Dru in a strangely disturbed state of mind, and all during the trip up from New York his thoughts were on Gloria and what the future would bring forth to them both.

On the afternoon following his arrival at the camp, as he and the young woman walked over the hills aflame with autumnal splendor, Gloria told of her bitter disappointment. The young man listened in sympathy, but after a long pause in which she saw him weighing the whole question in his mind, he said:

"Well, Gloria, so far as your work alone is concerned, there is something better that you can do if you will. The most important things to be done now are not amongst the poor but amongst the rich. There is where you may become a forceful missionary for good. All of us can reach the poor, for they welcome us, but there are only a few who think like you, who can reach the rich and powerful.

"Let that be your field of endeavor. Do your work gently and with moderation, so that some at least may listen. If we would convince and convert, we must veil our thoughts and curb our enthusiasm, so that those we would influence will think us reasonable."

"Well, Philip," answered Gloria, "if you really think I can help the cause, of course —"

"I'm sure you can help the cause. A lack of understanding is the chief obstacle, but, Gloria, you know that this is not an easy thing for me to say, for I realize that it will largely take you out of my life, for my path leads in the other direction.

"It will mean that I will no longer have you as a daily inspiration, and the sordidness and loneliness will press all the harder, but we have seen the true path, and now have a clearer understanding of the meaning and importance of our work."

"And so, Philip, it is decided that you will go back to the East Side to your destiny, and I will remain here, there and everywhere, Newport, New York, Palm Beach, London, carrying on my work as I see it."

They had wandered long and far by now, and had come again to the edge of the lofty forest that was a part of her father's estate. They stood for a moment in that vast silence looking into each other's eyes, and then they clasped hands over their tacit compact, and without a word, walked back to the bungalow.

CHAPTER XI

Selwyn Plots With Thor

FOR five years Gloria and Philip worked in their separate fields, but, nevertheless, coming in frequent touch with one another. Gloria proselyting the rich by showing them their selfishness, and turning them to a larger purpose in life, and Philip leading the forces of those who had consecrated themselves to the uplifting of the unfortunate. It did not take Philip long to discern that in the last analysis it would be necessary for himself and co-workers to reach the results aimed at through politics. Masterful and arrogant wealth, created largely by Government protection of its profits, not content with its domination and influence within a single party, had sought to corrupt them both, and to that end had insinuated itself into the primaries, in order that no candidates might be nominated whose views were not in accord with theirs.

By the use of all the money that could be spent, by a complete and compact organization and by the most infamous sort of deception regarding his real opinions and intentions, plutocracy had succeeded in electing its creature to the Presidency. There had been formed a league, the membership of which was composed of one thousand multi-millionaires, each one contributing ten thousand dollars. This gave a fund of ten million dollars with which to mislead those that could be misled, and to debauch the weak and uncertain.

This nefarious plan was conceived by a senator whose swollen fortune had been augmented year after year through the tributes paid him by the interests he represented. He had a marvelous aptitude for political manipulation and organization, and he forged a subtle chain with which to hold in subjection the natural impulses of the people. His plan was simple, but behind it was the cunning of a mind that had never known defeat. There was no man in either of the great political parties that was big enough to cope with him or to unmask his methods.

Up to the advent of Senator Selwyn, the interests had not successfully concealed their hands. Sometimes the public had been mistaken as to the true character of their officials, but sooner or later the truth had developed, for in most instances, wealth was openly for or against certain men and measures. But the adroit Selwyn moved differently.

His first move was to confer with John Thor, the high priest of finance, and unfold his plan to him, explaining how essential was secrecy. It was agreed between them that it should be known to the two of them only.

Thor's influence throughout commercial America was absolute. His wealth, his ability and even more the sum of the capital he could control through the banks, trust companies and industrial organizations, which he dominated, made his word as potent as that of a monarch.

He and Selwyn together went over the roll and selected the thousand that were to give each ten thousand dollars. Some they omitted for one reason or another, but when they had finished they had named those who could make or break within a day any man or corporation within their sphere of influence. Thor was to send for each of the thousand and compliment him that there was a matter, appertaining to the general welfare of the business fraternity, which needed twenty thousand dollars, that he, Thor, would put up ten, and wanted him to put up as much, that sometime in the future, or never, as the circumstances might require, would he make a report as to the expenditure and purpose therefor.

There were but few men of business between the Atlantic and Pacific, or between Canada and Mexico, who did not consider themselves fortunate in being called to New York by Thor, and in being asked to join him in a blind pool looking to the safeguarding of wealth. Consequently, the amassing of this great corruption fund in secret was simple. If necessity had demanded it twice the sum could have been raised.

The money when collected was placed in Thor's name in different banks controlled by him, and Thor, from time to time, as requested by Selwyn, placed in banks designated by him whatever sums were needed. Selwyn then transferred these amounts to the private bank of his son-in-law, who became final paymaster. The result was that the public had no chance of obtaining any knowledge of the fund or how it was spent.

The plan was simple, the result effective. Selwyn had no one to interfere with him. The members of the pool had contributed blindly to Thor, and Thor preferred not to know what Selwyn was doing nor how he did it. It was a one man power which in the hands of one possessing ability of the first class, is always potent for good or evil.

Not only did Selwyn plan to win the Presidency, but he also planned to bring under his control both the Senate and the Supreme Court. He selected one man in each of thirty of the States, some of them belonging to his party and some to the opposition, whom he intended to have run for the Senate.

If he succeeded in getting twenty of them elected, he counted upon having a good majority of the Senate, because there were already thirty-eight Senators upon whom he could rely in any serious attack upon corporate wealth.

As to the Supreme Court, of the nine justices there were three that were what he termed "safe and sane," and another that could be counted upon in a serious crisis.

Three of them, upon whom he could not rely, were of advanced age, and it was practically certain that the next President would have that many vacancies to fill. Then there would be an easy working majority.

His plan contemplated nothing further than this. His intention was to block all legislation adverse to the interests. He would have no new laws to fear, and of the old, the Supreme Court would properly interpret them.

He did not intend that his Senators should all vote alike, speak alike, or act from apparently similar motives. Where they came from States dominated by corporate wealth, he would have them frankly vote in the open, and according to their conviction.

When they came from agricultural States, where the sentiment was known as "progressive," they could cover their intentions in many ways. One method was by urging an amendment so radical that no honest progressive would consent to it, and then refusing to support the more moderate measure because it did not go far enough. Another was to inject some clause that was clearly unconstitutional, and insist upon its adoption, and refusing to vote for the bill without its insertion.

Selwyn had no intention of letting any one Senator know that he controlled any other senator. There were to be no caucuses, no conferences of his making, or anything that looked like an organization. He was the center, and from him radiated everything appertaining to measures affecting "the interests."

Chapter XII

Selwyn Seeks a Candidate

Selwyn then began carefully scrutinizing such public men in the States known as Presidential cradles, as seemed to him eligible. By a process of elimination he centered upon two that appeared desirable.

One was James R. Rockland, recently elected Governor of a State of the Middle West. The man had many of the earmarks of a demagogue, which Selwyn readily recognized, and he therefore concluded to try him first.

Accordingly he went to the capital of the State ostensibly upon private business, and dropped in upon the Governor in the most casual way. Rockland was distinctly flattered by the attention, for Selwyn was, perhaps, the best known figure in American politics, while he, himself, had only begun to attract attention. They had met at conventions and elsewhere, but they were practically unacquainted, for Rockland had never been permitted to enter the charmed circle which gathered around Selwyn.

"Good morning, Governor," said Selwyn, when he had been admitted to Rockland's private room. "I was passing through the capital and I thought I would look in on you and see how your official cares were using you."

"I am glad to see you, Senator," said Rockland effusively, "very glad, for there are some party questions coming up at the next session of the Legislature about which I particularly desire your advice."

"I have but a moment now, Rockland," answered the Senator, "but if you will dine with me in my rooms at the Mandell House to-night it will be a pleasure to talk over such matters with you."

"Thank you, Senator, at what hour?"

"You had better come at seven for if I finish my business here to-day, I shall leave on the 10 o'clock for Washington," said Selwyn.

Thus in the most casual way the meeting was arranged. As a matter of fact, Rockland had no party matters to discuss, and Selwyn knew it. He also knew that Rockland was ambitious to become a leader, and to get within the little group that controlled the party and the Nation.

Rockland was a man of much ability, but he fell far short of measuring up with Selwyn, who was in a class by himself. The Governor was a good orator, at times even brilliant, and while not a forceful man, yet he had magnetism which served him still better in furthering his political fortunes. He was not one that could be grossly corrupted, yet he was willing to play to the galleries in order to serve his ambition, and he was willing to forecast his political acts in order to obtain potential support.

When he reached the Mandell House, he was at once shown to the Senator's rooms. Selwyn received him cordially enough to be polite, and asked him if he would not look over the afternoon paper for a moment while he finished a note he was writing. He wrote leisurely, then rang for a boy and ordered dinner to be served.

Selwyn merely tasted the wine (he seldom did more) but Rockland drank freely though not to excess. After they had talked over the local matters which were supposed to be the purpose of the conference, much to Rockland's delight, the Senator began to discuss national politics.

"Rockland," began Selwyn, "can you hold this state in line at next year's election?"

"I feel sure that I can, Senator, why do you ask?"

"Since we have been talking here," he replied, "it has occurred to me that if you could be nominated and elected again, the party might do worse than to consider you for the presidential nomination the year following.

"No, my dear fellow, don't interrupt me," continued Selwyn mellifluously.

"It is strange how fate or chance enters into the life of man and even of nations. A business matter calls me here, I pass your office and think to pay my respects to the Governor of the State. Some political questions are perplexing you, and my presence suggests that I may aid in their solution. This dinner follows, your personality appeals to me, and the thought flits through my mind, why should not Rockland, rather than some other man, lead the party two years from now?

"And the result, my dear Rockland, may be, probably will be, your becoming chief magistrate of the greatest republic the sun has ever shone on."

Rockland by this time was fairly hypnotized by Selwyn's words, and by their tremendous import. For a moment he dared not trust himself to speak.

"Senator Selwyn," he said at last, "it would be idle for me to deny that you have excited within me an ambition that a moment ago would have seemed worse than folly. Your influence within the party and your ability to conduct a campaign, gives to your suggestion almost the tender of the presidency. To tell you that I am deeply moved does scant justice to my feelings. If, after further consideration, you think me worthy of the honor, I shall feel under lasting obligations to you which I shall endeavor to repay in every way consistent with honor and with a sacred regard for my oath of office."

"I want to tell you frankly, Rockland," answered Selwyn,

"that up to now I have had someone else in mind, but I am in no sense committed, and we might as well discuss the matter to as near a conclusion as is possible at this time."

Selwyn's voice hardened a little as he went on. "You would not want a nomination that could not carry with a reasonable certainty of election, therefore I would like to go over with you your record, both public and private, in the most open yet confidential way. It is better that you and I, in the privacy of these rooms, should lay bare your past than that it should be done in a bitter campaign and by your enemies. What we say to one another here is to be as if never spoken, and the grave itself must not be more silent. Your private life not only needs to be clean, but there must be no public act at which any one can point an accusing finger."

"Of course, of course," said Rockland, with a gesture meant to convey the complete openness of his record.

"Then comes the question of party regularity," continued Selwyn, without noticing. "Be candid with me, for, if you are not, the recoil will be upon your own head."

"I am sure that I can satisfy you on every point, Senator. I have never scratched a party ticket nor have I ever voted against any measure endorsed by a party caucus," said Governor Rockland.

"That is well," smiled the Senator. "I assume that in making your important appointments you will consult those of us who have stood sponsor for you, not only to the party but to the country. It would be very humiliating to me if I should insist upon your nomination and election and then should for four years have to apologize for what I had done."

Musingly, as if contemplating the divine presence in the works of man, Selwyn went on, while he closely watched Rockland from behind his half-closed eyelids.

"Our scheme of Government contemplates, I think, a diffuse responsibility, my dear Rockland. While a president has a constitutional right to act alone, he has no moral right to act contrary to the tenets and traditions of his party, or to the advice of the party leaders, for the country accepts the candidate, the party and the party advisers as a whole and not severally.

"It is a natural check, which by custom the country has endorsed as wise, and which must be followed in order to obtain a proper organization. Do you follow me, Governor, and do you endorse this unwritten law?"

If Rockland had heard this at second hand, if he had read it, or if it had related to someone other than himself, he would have detected the sophistry of it. But, exhilarated by wine and intoxicated by ambition, he saw nothing but a pledge to deal squarely by the organization.

"Senator," he replied fulsomely, "gratitude is one of the tenets of my religion, and therefore inversely ingratitude is unknown to me. You and the organization can count on my loyalty from the beginning to the end, for I shall never fail you.

"I know you will not ask me to do anything at which my conscience will rebel, nor to make an appointment that is not entirely fit."

"That, Rockland, goes without saying," answered the Senator with dignity. "I have all the wealth and all the position that I desire. I want nothing now except to do my share towards making my native land grow in prosperity, and to make the individual citizen more contented. To do this we must cease this eternal agitation, this constant proposal of half-baked measures, which the demagogues are offering as a panacea to all the ills that flesh is heir to.

"We need peace, legislative and political peace, so that our people may turn to their industries and work them to success, in the wholesome knowledge that the laws governing commerce and trade conditions will not be disturbed over night."

"I agree with you there, Senator," said Rockland eagerly.

"We have more new laws now than we can digest in a decade," continued Selwyn, "so let us have rest until we do digest them. In Europe the business world works under stable conditions. There we find no proposal to change the money system between moons, there we find no uncertainty from month to month regarding the laws under which manufacturers are to make their products, but with us, it is a wise man who knows when he can afford to enlarge his output.

"A high tariff threatens to-day, a low one to-morrow, and a large part of the time the business world lies in helpless perplexity.

"I take it, Rockland, that you are in favor of stability, that you will join me in my endeavors to give the country a chance to develop itself and its marvelous natural resources."

As a matter of fact, Rockland's career had given no evidence of such views. He had practically committed his political fortunes on the side of the progressives, but the world had turned around since then, and he viewed things differently.

"Senator," he said, his voice tense in his anxiety to prove his reliability, "I find that in the past I have taken only a cursory view of conditions. I see clearly that what you have outlined is a high order of statesmanship. You are constructive: I have been on the side of those who would tear down. I will gladly join hands with you and build up, so that the wealth and power of this country shall come to equal that of any two nations in existence."

Selwyn settled back in his chair, nodding his approval and telling himself that he would not need to seek further for his candidate.

At Rockland's earnest solicitation he remained over another day. The Governor gave him copies of his speeches and messages, so that he could assure himself that there was no serious flaw in his public record.

Selwyn cautioned him about changing his attitude too suddenly. "Go on, Rockland, as you have done in the past. It will not do to see the light too quickly. You have the progressives with you now, keep them, and I will let the conservatives know that you think straight and may be trusted.

"We must consult frequently together," he continued, "but cautiously. There is no need for any one to know that we are working together harmoniously. I may even get some of the conservative papers to attack you judiciously. It will not harm you. But, above all, do nothing of importance without consulting me.

"I am committing the party and the Nation to you, and my responsibility is a heavy one, and I owe it to them that no mistakes are made."

"You may trust me, Senator," said Rockland. "I understand perfectly."

CHAPTER XIII

Dru and Selwyn Meet

THE roads of destiny oftentimes lead us in strange and unlooked for directions and bring together those whose thoughts and purposes are as wide as space itself. When Gloria Strawn first entered boarding school, the roommate given her was Janet Selwyn, the youngest daughter of the Senator. They were alike in nothing, except, perhaps, in their fine perception of truth and honor. But they became devoted friends and had carried their attachment for one another beyond their school-girl days. Gloria was a frequent visitor at the Selwyn household both in Washington and Philadelphia, and was a favorite with the Senator. He often bantered her concerning her "socialistic views," and she in turn would declare that he would some day see the light. Now and then she let fall a hint of Philip, and one day Senator Selwyn suggested that she invite him over to Philadelphia to spend the week end with them. "Gloria, I would like to meet this paragon of the ages," said he jestingly, "although I am somewhat fearful that he may persuade me to 'sell all that I have and give it to the poor.'"

"I will promise to protect you during this one visit, Senator," said Gloria, "but after that I shall leave you to your fate."

"Dear Philip," wrote Gloria, "The great Senator Selwyn has expressed a wish to know you, and at his suggestion, I am writing to ask you here to spend with us the coming week end. I have promised that you will not denude him of all his possessions at your first meeting, but beyond that I have refused to go. Seriously, though, I think you should come, for if you would know something of politics, then why not get your lessons from the fountain head?

> "Your very sincere,
> "GLORIA."

In reply Philip wrote:

"Dear Gloria: You are ever anticipating my wishes. In the crusade we are making I find it essential to know politics, if we are to reach the final goal that we have in mind, and you have prepared the way for the first lesson. I will be over tomorrow on the four o'clock. Please do not bother to meet me.

> "Faithfully yours,
> "PHILIP."

Gloria and Janet Strawn were at the station to meet him. "Janet, this is Mr. Dru," said Gloria. "It makes me very happy to have my two best friends meet." As they got in her electric runabout, Janet Strawn said, "Since dinner will not be served for two hours or more, let us drive in the park for a while." Gloria was pleased to see that Philip was interested in the bright, vivacious chatter of her friend, and she was glad to hear him respond in the same light strain. However, she was confessedly nervous when Senator Selwyn and Philip met. Though in different ways, she admired them both profoundly. Selwyn had a delightful personality, and Gloria felt sure that Philip would come measurably under the influence of it, even though their views were so widely divergent. And in this she was right. Here, she felt, were two great antagonists, and she was eager for the intellectual battle to begin. But she was to be disappointed, for Philip became the listener, and did but little of the talking. He led Senator Selwyn into a dissertation upon the present conditions of the country, and the bearing of the political questions upon them. Selwyn said nothing indiscreet, yet he unfolded to Philip's view a new and potential world. Later in the evening, the Senator was unsuccessful in his efforts to draw from his young guest his point of view. Philip saw the futility of such a discussion, and contented Selwyn by expressing an earnest appreciation of his patience in making clear so many things about which he had been ignorant. Next morning, Senator Selwyn was strolling with Gloria in the rose garden, when he said, "Gloria, I like your friend Dru. I do not recall ever having met anyone like him." "Then you got him to talk after we left last night. I am so glad. I was afraid he had on one of his quiet spells."

"No, he said but little, but the questions he asked gave me glimpses of his mind that sometimes startled me. He was polite, modest but elusive, nevertheless, I like him, and shall see more of him." Far sighted as Selwyn was, he did not know the full extent of this prophecy.

CHAPTER XIV

The Making of a President

SELWYN now devoted himself to the making of enough conservative senators to control comfortably that body. The task was not difficult to a man of his sagacity with all the money he could spend.

Newspapers were subsidized in ways they scarcely recognized themselves. Honest officials who were in the way were removed by offering them places vastly more remunerative, and in this manner he built up a strong, intelligent and well constructed machine. It was done so sanely and so quietly that no one suspected the master mind behind it all. Selwyn was responsible to no one, took no one into his confidence, and was therefore in no danger of betrayal.

It was a fascinating game to Selwyn. It appealed to his intellectual side far more than it did to his avarice. He wanted to govern the Nation with an absolute hand, and yet not be known as the directing power. He arranged to have his name appear less frequently in the press and he never submitted to interviews, laughingly ridding himself of reporters by asserting that he knew nothing of importance. He had a supreme contempt for the blatant self-advertised politician, and he removed himself as far as possible from that type.

In the meantime his senators were being elected, the Rockland sentiment was steadily growing and his nomination was finally brought about by the progressives fighting vigorously for him and the conservatives yielding a reluctant consent. It was done so adroitly that Rockland would have been fooled himself, had not Selwyn informed him in advance of each move as it was made.

After the nomination, Selwyn had trusted men put in charge of the campaign, which he organized himself, though largely under cover. The opposition party had every reason to believe that they would be successful, and it was a great intellectual treat to Selwyn to overcome their natural advantages by the sheer force of ability, plus what money he needed to carry out his plans. He put out the cry of lack of funds, and indeed it seemed to be true, for he was too wise to make a display of his resources. To ward heelers, to the daily press, and to professional stump speakers, he gave scant comfort. It was not to such sources that he looked for success.

He began by eliminating all states he knew the opposition party would certainly carry, but he told the party leaders there to claim that a revolution was brewing, and that a landslide would follow at the election. This would keep the antagonists busy and make them less effective elsewhere.

He also ignored the states where his side was sure to win. In this way he was free to give his entire thoughts to the twelve states that were debatable, and upon whose votes the election would turn. He divided each of these states into units containing five thousand voters, and, at the national headquarters, he placed one man in charge of each unit. Of the five thousand, he roughly calculated there would be two thousand voters that no kind of persuasion could turn from his party and two thousand that could not be changed from the opposition. This would leave one thousand doubtful ones to win over. So he had a careful poll made in each unit, and eliminated the strictly unpersuadable party men, and got down to a complete analysis of the debatable one thousand. Information was obtained as to their race, religion, occupation and former political predilection. It was easy then to know how to reach each individual by literature, by persuasion or perhaps by some more subtle argument. No mistake was made by sending the wrong letter or the wrong man to any of the desired one thousand.

In the states so divided, there was, at the local headquarters, one man for each unit just as at the national headquarters. So these two had only each other to consider, and their duty was to bring to Rockland a majority of the one thousand votes within their charge. The local men gave the conditions, the national men gave the proper literature and advice, and the local man then applied it. The money that it cost to maintain such an organization was more than saved from the waste that would have occurred under the old method.

The opposition management was sending out tons of printed matter, but they sent it to state headquarters that, in turn, distributed it to the county organizations, where it was dumped into a corner and given to visitors when asked for. Selwyn's committee used one-fourth as much printed matter, but it went in a sealed envelope, along with a cordial letter, direct to a voter that had as yet not decided how he would vote.

The opposition was sending speakers at great expense from one end of the country to the other, and the sound of their voices rarely fell on any but friendly and sympathetic ears. Selwyn sent men into his units to personally persuade each of the one thousand hesitating voters to support the Rockland ticket.

The opposition was spending large sums upon the daily press. Selwyn used the weekly press so that he could reach the fireside of every farmer and the dweller in the small country towns. These were the ones that would read every line in their local papers and ponder over it.

The opposition had its candidates going by special train to every part of the Union, making many speeches every day, and mostly to voters that could not be driven from him either by force or persuasion. The leaders in cities, both large and small, would secure a date and, having in mind for themselves a postmastership or collectorship, would tell their followers to turn out in great force and give the candidate a big ovation. They wanted the candidate to remember the enthusiasm of these places, and to leave greatly pleased and under the belief that he was making untold converts. As a matter of fact his voice would seldom reach any but a staunch partisan.

Selwyn kept Rockland at home, and arranged to have him meet by special appointment the important citizens of the twelve uncertain states. He would have the most prominent party leader, in a particular state, go to a rich brewer or large manufacturer, whose views had not yet been crystallized, and say, "Governor Rockland has expressed a desire to know you, and I would like to arrange a meeting." The man approached would be flattered to think he was of such importance that a candidate for the presidency had expressed a desire to meet him. He would know it was his influence that was wanted but, even so, there was a subtle flattery in that. An appointment would be arranged. Just before he came into Rockland's presence, his name and a short epitome of his career would be handed to Rockland to read. When he reached Rockland's home he would at first be denied admittance. His sponsor would say, "this is Mr. Munting of Muntingville." "Oh, pardon me, Mr. Munting, Governor Rockland expects you."

And in this way he is ushered into the presence of the great. His fame, up to a moment ago, was unknown to Rockland, but he now grasps his hand cordially and says — "I am delighted to know you, Mr. Munting. I recall the address you made a few years ago when you gave a library to Muntingville. It is men of your type that have made America what it is to-day, and, whether you support me or not, if I am elected President it is such as you that I hope will help sustain my hands in my effort to give to our people a clean, sane and conservative government."

When Munting leaves he is stepping on air. He sees visions of visits to Washington to consult the President upon matters of state, and perhaps he sees an ambassadorship in the misty future. He becomes Rockland's ardent supporter, and his purse is open and his influence is used to the fullest extent.

And this was Selwyn's way. It was all so simple. The opposition was groaning under the thought of having one hundred millions of people to reach, and of having to persuade a majority of twenty millions of voters to take their view.

Selwyn had only one thousand doubtful voters in each of a few units on his mind, and he knew the very day when a majority of them had decided to vote for Rockland, and that his fight was won. The pay-roll of the opposition was filled with incompetent political hacks, that had been fastened upon the management by men of influence. Selwyn's force, from end to end, was composed of able men who did a full day's work under the eye of their watchful taskmaster.

And Selwyn won and Rockland became the keystone of the arch he had set out to build.

There followed in orderly succession the inauguration, the selection of cabinet officers and the new administration was launched.

Drunk with power and the adulation of sycophants, once or twice Rockland asserted himself, and acted upon important matters without having first conferred with Selwyn. But, after he had been bitterly assailed by Selwyn's papers and by his senators, he made no further attempts at independence. He felt that he was utterly helpless in that strong man's hands, and so, indeed, he was.

One of the Supreme Court justices died, two retired because of age, and all were replaced by men suggested by Selwyn.

He now had the Senate, the Executive and a majority of the Court of last resort. The government was in his hands. He had reached the summit of his ambition, and the joy of it made all his work seem worth while.

But Selwyn, great man that he was, did not know, could not know, that when his power was greatest it was most insecure. He did not know, could not know, what force was working to his ruin and to the ruin of his system.

Take heart, therefore, you who had lost faith in the ultimate destiny of the Republic, for a greater than Selwyn is here to espouse your cause. He comes panoplied in justice and with the light of reason in his eyes. He comes as the advocate of equal opportunity and he comes with the power to enforce his will.

CHAPTER XV

The Exultant Conspirators

IT WAS a strange happening, the way the disclosure was made and the Nation came to know of the Selwyn-Thor conspiracy to control the government.

Thor, being without any delicate sense of honor, was in the habit of using a dictagraph to record what was intended to be confidential conversations. He would take these confidential records, clearly mark them, and place them in his private safe within the vault. When the transaction to which they related was closed he destroyed them.

The character of the instrument was carefully concealed. It was a part of a massive piece of office furniture, which answered for a table as well. In order to facilitate his correspondence, he often used it for dictating, and no one but Thor knew that it was ever put into commission for other purposes.

He had never, but once, had occasion to use a record that related to a private conversation or agreement. Then it concerned a matter involving a large sum, a demand having been made upon him that smacked of blackmail. He arranged a meeting, which his opponent regarded as an indication that he was willing to yield. There were present the contestant, his lawyer, Thor's counsel and Thor himself.

"Before discussing the business that is before us," said Thor, "I think you would all enjoy, more or less, a record which I have in my dictagraph, and which I have just listened to with a great deal of pleasure."

He handed a tube to each and started the machine. It is a pity that Hogarth could not have been present to have painted the several expressions that came upon the faces of those four. A quiet but amused satisfaction beamed from Thor, and his counsel could not conceal a broad smile, but the wretched victim was fairly sick from mortification and defeated avarice. He finally could stand no more and took the tube from his ear, reached for his hat and was gone.

Thor had not seen Selwyn for a long time, but one morning, when he was expecting another for whom he had his dictagraph set, Selwyn was announced. He asked him in and gave orders that they were not to be disturbed. When Selwyn had assured himself that they were absolutely alone he told Thor his whole story.

It was of absorbing interest, and Thor listened fairly hypnotized by the recital, which at times approached the dramatic. It was the first time that Selwyn had been able to unbosom himself, and he enjoyed the impression he was making upon the great financier. When he told how Rockland had made an effort for freedom and how he brought him back, squirming under his defeat, they laughed joyously.

Rich though he was beyond the dreams of avarice, rich as no man had ever before been, Thor could not refrain from a mental calculation of how enormously such a situation advanced his fortune. There was to be no restriction now, he could annihilate and absorb at will. He had grown so powerful that his mental equilibrium was unbalanced upon the question of accretion. He wanted more, he must have more, and now, by the aid of Selwyn, he would have more. He was so exultant that he gave some expression to his thoughts, and Selwyn, cynical as he was, was shocked and began to fear the consequences of his handiwork.

He insisted upon Selwyn's lunching with him in order to celebrate the triumph of "their" plan. Selwyn was amused at the plural. They went to a near-by club and remained for several hours talking of things of general interest, for Selwyn refused to discuss his victory after they had left the protecting walls of Thor's office.

Thor had forgotten his other engagement, and along with it he forgot the dictagraph that he had set. When he returned to his office he could not recall whether or not he had set the dictagraph. He looked at it, saw that it was not set, but that here was an unused record in it and dismissed it from his mind. He wanted no more business for the day. He desired to get out and walk and think and enjoy the situation. And so he went, a certain unholy joy within his warped and money-soddened heart.

CHAPTER XVI

The Exposure

LONG after Thor had gone, long after the day had dwindled into twilight and the twilight had shaded into dusk, Thomas Spears, his secretary sat and pondered. After Thor and Selwyn had left the office for luncheon he had gone to the dictagraph to see whether there was anything for him to take. He found the record, saw it had been used, removed it to his machine and got ready to transmit. He was surprised to find that it was Selwyn's voice that came to him, then Thor's, and again Selwyn's. He knew then that it was not intended for dictation, that there was some mistake and yet he held it until he had gotten the whole of the mighty conspiracy. Pale and greatly agitated he remained motionless for a long time. Then he returned to Thor's office, placed a new record in the machine and closed it.

Spears came from sturdy New England stock and was at heart a patriot. He had come to New York largely by accident of circumstances.

Spears had a friend named Harry Tracy, with whom he had grown up in the little Connecticut village they called home, and who was distantly related to Thor, whose forebears also came from that vicinity. They had gone to the same commercial school, and were trained particularly in stenography and typing. Tracy sought and obtained a place in Thor's office. He was attentive to his duties, very accurate, and because of his kinship and trustworthiness, Thor made him his confidential secretary. The work became so heavy that Tracy got permission to employ an assistant. He had Spears in mind for the place, and, after conferring with Thor, offered it to him.

Thor consented largely because he preferred some one who had not lived in New York, and was in no way entangled with the life and sentiment of the city. Being from New England himself, he trusted the people of that section as he did no others.

So Thomas Spears was offered the place and gladly accepted it. He had not been there long before he found himself doing all the stenographic work and typing.

Spears was a man of few words. He did his work promptly and well. Thor had him closely shadowed for a long while, and the report came that he had no bad habits and but few companions and those of the best. But Thor could get no confidential report upon the workings of his mind. He did not know that his conscience sickened at what he learned through the correspondence and from his fellow clerks. He did not know that his every heart beat was for the unfortunate that came within the reach of Thor's avarice, and were left the merest derelicts upon the financial seas.

All the clerks were gone, the lights were out and Spears sat by the window looking out over the great modern Babylon, still fighting with his conscience. His sense of loyalty to the man who gave him his livelihood rebelled at the thought of treachery. It was not unlike accepting food and shelter and murdering your benefactor, for Spears well knew that in the present state of the public mind if once the truth were known, it would mean death to such as Thor. For with a fatuous ignorance of public feeling the interests had gone blindly on, conceding nothing, stifling competition and absorbing the wealth and energies of the people.

Spears knew that the whole social and industrial fabric of the nation was at high tension, and that it needed but a spark to explode. He held within his hand that spark. Should he plunge the country, his country, into a bloody internecine war, or should he let the Selwyns and the Thors trample the hopes, the fortunes and the lives of the people under foot for still another season. If he held his peace it did but postpone the conflict.

The thought flashed through his mind of the bigness of the sum any one of the several great dailies would give to have the story. And then there followed a sense of shame that he could think of such a thing.

He felt that he was God's instrument for good and that he should act accordingly. He was aroused now, he would no longer parley with his conscience. What was best to do? That was the only question left to debate.

He looked at an illuminated clock upon a large white shaft that lifted its marble shoulders towards the stars. It was nine o'clock. He turned on the lights, ran over the telephone book until he reached the name of what he considered the most important daily. He said: "Mr. John Thor's office desires to speak with the Managing Editor." This at once gave him the connection he desired.

"This is Mr. John Thor's secretary, and I would like to see you immediately upon a matter of enormous public importance. May I come to your office at once?"

There was something in the voice that startled the newspaper man, and he wondered what Thor's office could possibly want with him concerning any matter, public or private. However, he readily consented to an interview and waited with some impatience for the quarter of an hour to go by that was necessary to cover the distance. He gave orders to have Spears brought in as soon as he arrived.

When Spears came he told the story with hesitation and embarrassment. The Managing Editor thought at first that he was in the presence of a lunatic, but after a few questions he began to believe. He had a dictagraph in his office and asked for the record. He was visibly agitated when the full import of the news became known to him. Spears insisted that the story be given to all the city newspapers and to the Associated Press, which the Managing Editor promised to do.

When the story was read the next morning by America's millions, it was clear to every farsighted person that a crisis had come and that revolution was imminent. Men at once divided themselves into groups. Now, as it has ever been, the very poor largely went with the rich and powerful. The reason for this may be partly from fear and partly from habit. They had seen the struggle going on for centuries and with but one result.

A mass meeting was called to take place the day following at New York's largest public hall. The call was not inflammatory, but asked "all good citizens to lend their counsel and influence to the rectification of those abuses that had crept into the Government," and it was signed by many of the best known men in the Nation.

The hall was packed to its limits an hour before the time named. A distinguished college president from a nearby town was given the chair, and in a few words he voiced the indignation and the humiliation which they all felt. Then one speaker after another bitterly denounced the administration, and advocated the overthrow of the Government. One, more intemperate than the rest, urged an immediate attack on Thor and all his kind. This was met by a roar of approval.

Philip had come early and was seated well in front. In the pandemonium that now prevailed no speaker could be heard. Finally Philip fought his way to the stage, gave his name to the chairman, and asked to be heard.

When the white-haired college president arose there was a measure of quiet, and when he mentioned Philip's name and they saw his splendid, homely face there was a curious hush. He waited for nearly a minute after perfect quiet prevailed, and then, in a voice like a deep-toned bell, he spoke with such fervor and eloquence that one who was present said afterwards that he knew the hour and the man had come. Philip explained that hasty and ill-considered action had ruined other causes as just as theirs, and advised moderation. He suggested that a committee be named by the chairman to draw up a plan of procedure, to be presented at another meeting to be held the following night. This was agreed to, and the chairman received tremendous applause when he named Philip first.

This meeting had been called so quickly, and the names attached to the call were so favorably known, that the country at large seemed ready to wait upon its conclusions.

It was apparent from the size and earnestness of the second gathering that the interest was growing rather than abating.

Philip read the plan which his committee had formulated, and then explained more at length their reasons for offering it. Briefly, it advised no resort to violence, but urged immediate organization and cooperation with citizens throughout the United States who were in sympathy with the movement. He told them that the conscience of the people was now aroused, and that there would be no halting until the Government was again within their hands to be administered for the good of the many instead of for the good of a rapacious few.

The resolutions were sustained, and once more Philip was placed at the head of a committee to perfect not only a state, but a national organization as well. Calls for funds to cover preliminary expense brought immediate and generous response, and the contest was on.

CHAPTER XVII

Selwyn and Thor Defend Themselves

IN THE meantime Selwyn and Thor had issued an address, defending their course as warranted by both the facts and the law.

They said the Government had been honeycombed by irresponsible demagogues, that were fattening upon the credulity of the people to the great injury of our commerce and prosperity, that no laws unfriendly to the best interests had been planned, and no act had been contemplated inconsistent with the dignity and honor of the Nation. They contended that in protecting capital against vicious assaults, they were serving the cause of labor and advancing the welfare of all.

Thor's whereabouts was a mystery, but Selwyn, brave and defiant, pursued his usual way.

President Rockland also made a statement defending his appointments of Justices of the Supreme Court, and challenged anyone to prove them unfit. He said that, from the foundation of the Government, it had become customary for a President to make such appointments from amongst those whose views were in harmony with his own, that in this case he had selected men of well known integrity, and of profound legal ability, and, because they were such, they were brave enough to stand for the right without regard to the clamor of ill-advised and ignorant people. He stated that he would continue to do his duty, and that he would uphold the constitutional rights of all the people without distinction to race, color or previous condition.

Acting under Selwyn's advice, Rockland began to concentrate quietly troops in the large centers of population. He also ordered the fleets into home waters. A careful inquiry was made regarding the views of the several Governors within easy reach of Washington, and, finding most of them favorable to the Government, he told them that in case of disorder he would honor their requisition for federal troops. He advised a thorough overlooking of the militia, and the weeding out of those likely to sympathize with the "mob." If trouble came, he promised to act promptly and forcefully, and not to let mawkish sentiment encourage further violence.

He recalled to them that the French Revolution was caused, and continued, by the weakness and inertia of Louis Fifteenth and his ministers and that the moment the Directorate placed Bonaparte in command of a handful of troops, and gave him power to act, by the use of grape and ball he brought order in a day. It only needed a quick and decisive use of force, he thought, and untold suffering and bloodshed would be averted.

President Rockland believed what he said. He seemed not to know that Bonaparte dealt with a ragged, ignorant mob, and had back of him a nation that had been in a drunken and bloody orgy for a period of years and wanted to sober up. He seemed not to know that in this contest, the clear-brained, sturdy American patriot was enlisted against him and what he represented, and had determined to come once more into his own.

CHAPTER XVIII

Gloria's Work Bears Fruit

IN HER efforts toward proselyting the rich, Gloria had not neglected her immediate family. By arguments and by bringing to the fore concrete examples to illustrate them, she had succeeded in awakening within her father a curious and unhappy frame of mind. That shifting and illusive thing we call conscience was beginning to assert itself in divers ways.

The first glimpse that Gloria had of his change of heart was at a dinner party. The discussion began by a dyspeptic old banker declaring that before the business world could bring the laboring classes to their senses it would be necessary to shut down the factories for a time and discontinue new enterprises in order that their dinner buckets and stomachs might become empty.

Before Gloria could take up the cudgels in behalf of those seeking a larger share of the profits of their labor, Mr. Strawn had done so. The debate between the two did not last long and was not unduly heated, but Gloria knew that the Rubicon had been crossed and that in the future she would have a powerful ally in her father.

Neither had she been without success in other directions, and she was, therefore, able to report to Philip very satisfactory progress. In one of their many conferences she was glad to be able to tell him that in the future abundant financial backing was assured for any cause recommended by either of them as being worthy. This was a long step forward, and Philip congratulated Gloria upon her efficient work.

"Do you remember, Gloria," he said, "how unhappy you were over the thought of laboring among the rich instead of the poor? And yet, contemplate the result. You have not only given some part of your social world an insight into real happiness, but you are enabling the balance of us to move forward at a pace that would have been impossible without your aid."

Gloria flushed with pleasure at his generous praise and replied: "It is good of you, Philip, to give me so large a credit, and I will not deny that I am very happy over the outcome of my endeavors, unimportant though they be. I am so glad, Philip, that you have been given the leadership of our side in the coming struggle, for I shall now feel confident of success."

"Do not be too sure, Gloria. We have the right and a majority of the American people with us; yet, on the other hand, we have opposed to us not only resourceful men but the machinery of a great Government buttressed by unlimited wealth and credit."

"Why could not I 'try out' the sincerity of my rich converts and get them to help finance your campaign?"

"Happy thought! If you succeed in doing that, Gloria, you will become the Joan d'Arc of our cause, and unborn generations will hold you in grateful remembrance."

"How you do enthuse one, Philip. I feel already as if my name were written high upon the walls of my country's Valhalla. Tell me how great a fund you will require, and I will proceed at once to build the golden ladder upon which I am to climb to fame."

"You need not make light of your suggestion in this matter, Gloria, for the lack of funds with which to organize is essentially our weakest point. With money we can overthrow the opposition, without it I am afraid they may defeat us. As to the amount needed, I can set no limit. The more you get the more perfectly can we organize. Do what you can and do it quickly, and be assured that if the sum is considerable and if our cause triumphs, you will have been the most potent factor of us all."

And then they parted; Gloria full of enthusiasm over her self-appointed task, and Philip with a silent prayer for her success.

CHAPTER XIX

War Clouds Hover

GLORIA was splendidly successful in her undertaking and within two weeks she was ready to place at Philip's disposal an amount far in excess of anything he had anticipated.

"It was so easy that I have a feeling akin to disappointment that I did not have to work harder," she wrote in her note to Philip announcing the result. "When I explained the purpose and the importance of the outcome, almost everyone approached seemed eager to have a share in the undertaking."

In his reply of thanks, Philip said, "The sum you have realized is far beyond any figure I had in mind. With what we have collected throughout the country, it is entirely sufficient, I think, to effect a preliminary organization, both political and military. If the final result is to be civil war, then the states that cast their fortunes with ours, will, of necessity, undertake the further financing of the struggle."

Philip worked assiduously upon his organization. It was first intended to make it political and educational, but when the defiant tone of Selwyn, Thor and Rockland was struck, and their evident intention of using force became apparent, he almost wholly changed it into a military organization. His central bureau was now in touch with every state, and he found in the West a grim determination to bring matters to a conclusion as speedily as possible.

On the other hand, he was sparring for time. He knew his various groups were in no condition to be pitted against any considerable number of trained regulars. He hoped, too, that actual conflict would be avoided, and that a solution could be arrived at when the forthcoming election for representatives occurred.

It was evident that a large majority of the people were with them: the problem was to get a fair and legal expression of opinion. As yet, there was no indication that this would not be granted.

The preparations on both sides became so open, that there was no longer any effort to work under cover. Philip cautioned his adherents against committing any overt act. He was sure that the administration forces would seize the slightest pretext to precipitate action, and that, at this time, would give them an enormous advantage.

He himself trained the men in his immediate locality, and he also had the organization throughout the country trained, but without guns. The use of guns would not have been permitted except to regular authorized militia. The drilling was done with wooden guns, each man hewing out a stick to the size and shape of a modern rifle. At his home, carefully concealed, each man had his rifle.

And then came the election. Troops were at the polls and a free ballot was denied. It was the last straw. Citizens gathering after nightfall in order to protest were told to disperse immediately, and upon refusal, were fired upon. The next morning showed a death roll in the large centers of population that was appalling.

Wisconsin was the state in which there was the largest percentage of the citizenship unfavorable to the administration and to the interests. Iowa, Minnesota and Nebraska were closely following.

Philip concluded to make his stand in the West, and he therefore ordered the men in every organization east of the Mississippi to foregather at once at Madison, and to report to him there. He was in constant touch with those Governors who were in sympathy with the progressive or insurgent cause, and he wired the Governor of Wisconsin, in cipher, informing him of his intentions.

As yet travel had not been seriously interrupted, though business was largely at a standstill, and there was an ominous quiet over the land. The opposition misinterpreted this, and thought that the people had been frightened by the unexpected show of force. Philip knew differently, and he also knew that civil war had begun. He communicated his plans to no one, but he had the campaign well laid out. It was his intention to concentrate in Wisconsin as large a force as could be gotten from his followers east and south of that state, and to concentrate again near Des Moines every man west of Illinois whom he could enlist. It was his purpose then to advance simultaneously both bodies of troops upon Chicago.

In the south there had developed a singular inertia. Neither side counted upon material help or opposition there.

The great conflict covering the years from 1860 to 1865 was still more than a memory, though but few living had taken part in it. The victors in that mighty struggle thought they had been magnanimous to the defeated but the well-informed Southerner knew that they had been made to pay the most stupendous penalty ever exacted in modern times. At one stroke of the pen, two thousand millions of their property was taken from them. A pension system was then inaugurated that taxed the resources of the Nation to pay. By the year 1927 more than five thousand millions had gone to those who were of the winning side. Of this the South was taxed her part, receiving nothing in return.

Cynical Europe said that the North would have it appear that a war had been fought for human freedom, whereas it seemed that it was fought for money. It forgot the many brave and patriotic men who enlisted because they held the Union to be one and indissoluble, and were willing to sacrifice their lives to make it so, and around whom a willing and grateful government threw its protecting arms. And it confused those deserving citizens with the unworthy many, whom pension agents and office seekers had debauched at the expense of the Nation. Then, too, the South remembered that one of the immediate results of emancipation was that millions of ignorant and indigent people were thrown upon the charity and protection of the Southern people, to care for and to educate. In some states sixty per cent. of the population were negroes, and they were as helpless as children and proved a heavy burden upon the forty per cent. of whites.

In rural populations more schoolhouses had to be maintained, and more teachers employed for the number taught, and the percentage of children per capita was larger than in cities. Then, of necessity, separate schools had to be maintained. So, altogether, the load was a heavy one for an impoverished people to carry.

The humane, the wise, the patriotic thing to have done, was for the Nation to have assumed the responsibility of the education of the Negroes for at least one generation.

What a contrast we see in England's treatment of the Boers. After a long and bloody war, which drew heavily upon the lives and treasures of the Nation, England's first act was to make an enormous grant to the conquered Boers, that they might have every facility to regain their shattered fortunes, and bring order and prosperity to their distracted land.

We see the contrast again in that for nearly a half century after the Civil War was over, no Southerner was considered eligible for the Presidency.

On the other hand, within a few years after the African Revolution ended, a Boer General, who had fought throughout the war with vigor and distinction, was proposed and elected Premier of the United Colonies.

Consequently, while sympathizing with the effort to overthrow Selwyn's government, the South moved slowly and with circumspection.

CHAPTER XX

Civil War Begins

GENERAL DRU brought together an army of fifty thousand men at Madison and about forty thousand near Des Moines, and recruits were coming in rapidly.

President Rockland had concentrated twenty thousand regulars and thirty thousand militia at Chicago, and had given command to Major General Newton, he who, several years previously, won the first medal given by the War Department for the best solution of the military problem.

The President also made a call for two hundred thousand volunteers. The response was in no way satisfactory, so he issued a formal demand upon each state to furnish its quota.

The states that were in sympathy with his administration responded, the others ignored the call.

General Dru learned that large reënforcements had been ordered to Chicago, and he therefore at once moved upon that place. He had a fair equipment of artillery, considering he was wholly dependent upon that belonging to the militia of those states that had ranged themselves upon his side, and at several points in the West, he had seized factories and plants making powder, guns, clothing and camp equipment. He ordered the Iowa division to advance at the same time, and the two forces were joined at a point about fifty miles south of Chicago.

General Newton was daily expecting reënforcements, but they failed to reach him before Dru made it impossible for them to pass through.

Newton at first thought to attack the Iowa division and defeat it, and then meet the Wisconsin division, but he hesitated to leave Chicago lest Dru should take the place during his ab-

97

sence.

With both divisions united, and with recruits constantly arriving, Dru had an army of one hundred and fifty thousand men.

Failing to obtain the looked-for reënforcements and seeing the hopelessness of opposing so large a force, Newton began secretly to evacuate Chicago by way of the Lakes, Dru having completely cut him off by land.

He succeeded in removing his army to Buffalo, where President Rockland had concentrated more than one hundred thousand troops.

When Dru found General Newton had evacuated Chicago, he occupied it, and then moved further east, in order to hold the states of Michigan, Indiana and Western Ohio.

This gave him the control of the West, and he endeavored as nearly as possible to cut off the food supply of the East. In order to tighten further the difficulty of obtaining supplies, he occupied Duluth and all the Lake ports as far east as Cleveland, which city the Government held, and which was their furthest western line.

Canada was still open as a means of food supply to the East, as were all the ports of the Atlantic seaboard as far south as Charleston.

So the sum of the situation was that the East, so far west as the middle of Ohio, and as far south as West Virginia, inclusive of that state, was in the hands of the Government.

Western Ohio, Indiana, Michigan and Illinois, while occupied by General Dru, were divided in their sympathies. Wisconsin, Minnesota, and every state west of the Mississippi, were strongly against the Government.

The South, as a whole, was negligible, though Virginia, Kentucky, Tennessee and Missouri were largely divided in sentiment. That part of the South lying below the border states was in sympathy with the insurgents.

The contest had come to be thought of as a conflict between Senator Selwyn on the one hand, and what he represented, and Philip Dru on the other, and what he stood for. These two were known to be the dominating forces on either side.

The contestants, on the face of things, seemed not unevenly matched, but, as a matter of fact, the conscience of the great mass of the people, East and West, was on Dru's side, for it was known that he was contending for those things which would permit the Nation to become again a land of freedom in its truest and highest sense, a land of equal opportunity, a land where justice would be meted out alike to the high and low with a steady and impartial hand.

CHAPTER XXI

Upon the Eve of Battle

NEITHER side seemed anxious to bring matters to a conclusion, for both Newton and Dru required time to put their respective armies in fit condition before risking a conflict.

By the middle of July, Dru had more than four hundred thousand men under his command, but his greatest difficulty was to properly officer and equip them. The bulk of the regular army officers had remained with the Government forces, though there were some notable exceptions. Among those offering their services to Dru was Jack Strawn. He resigned from the regular army with many regrets and misgivings, but his devotion to Philip made it impossible for him to do otherwise. And then there was Gloria whom he loved dearly, and who made him feel that there was a higher duty then mere professional regularity.

None of Dru's generals had been tried out in battle, and, indeed, he himself had not. It was much the same with the Government forces, for there had been no war since that with Spain in the nineties, and that was an affair so small it afforded but little training for either officers or men.

Dru had it in mind to make the one battle decisive, if that were possible of accomplishment, for he did not want to weaken and distract the country by such a conflict as that of 1861 to 1865.

The Government forces numbered six hundred thousand men under arms, but one hundred thousand of these were widely scattered in order to hold certain sections of the country in line.

On the first of September General Dru began to move towards the enemy. He wanted to get nearer Washington and the northern seaboard cities, so that if successful he would be within striking distance of them before the enemy could recover.

He had in mind the places he preferred the battle to occur, and he used all his skill in bringing about the desired result. As he moved slowly but steadily towards General Newton, he was careful not to tax the strength of his troops, but he desired to give them the experience in marching they needed, and also to harden them.

The civilized nations of the world had agreed not to use in war aeroplanes or any sort of air craft either as engines of destruction or for scouting purposes. This decision had been brought about by the International Peace Societies and by the self-evident impossibility of using them without enormous loss of life. Therefore none were being used by either the Government or insurgent forces.

General Newton thought that Dru was planning to attack him at a point about twenty miles west of Buffalo, where he had his army stretched from the Lake eastward, and where he had thrown up entrenchments and otherwise prepared for battle.

But Dru had no thought of attacking then or there, but moved slowly and orderly on until the two armies were less than twenty miles apart due north and south from one another.

When he continued marching eastward and began to draw away from General Newton, the latter for the first time realized that he himself would be compelled to pursue and attack, for the reason that he could not let Dru march upon New York and the other unprotected seaboard cities. He saw, too, that he had been out-generaled, and that he should have thrown his line across Dru's path and given battle at a point of his own choosing.

The situation was a most unusual one even in the complex

history of warfare, because in case of defeat the loser would be forced to retreat into the enemies' country. It all the more surely emphasized the fact that one great battle would determine the war. General Dru knew from the first what must follow his movement in marching by General Newton, and since he had now reached the ground that he had long chosen as the place where he wished the battle to occur, he halted and arranged his troops in formation for the expected attack.

There was a curious feeling of exultation and confidence throughout the insurgent army, for Dru had conducted every move in the great game with masterly skill, and no man was ever more the idol of his troops, or of the people whose cause he was the champion.

It was told at every camp fire in his army how he had won the last medal that had been given by the War Department and for which General Newton had been a contestant, and not one of his men doubted that as a military genius, Newton in no way measured up to Dru. It was plain that Newton had been outmaneuvered and that the advantage lay with the insurgent forces.

The day before the expected battle, General Dru issued a stirring address, which was placed in the hands of each soldier, and which concluded as follows: — "It is now certain that there will be but one battle, and its result lies with you. If you fight as I know you will fight, you surely will be successful, and you soon will be able to return to your homes and to your families, carrying with you the assurance that you have won what will be perhaps the most important victory that has ever been achieved. It is my belief that human liberty has never more surely hung upon the outcome of any conflict than it does upon this, and I have faith that when you are once ordered to advance, you will never turn back. If you will each make a resolution to conquer or die, you will not only conquer, but our death list will not be nearly so heavy as if you at any time falter."

This address was received with enthusiasm, and comrade declared to comrade that there would be no turning back when once called upon to advance, and it was a compact that in honor could not be broken. This, then, was the situation upon the eve of the mighty conflict.

CHAPTER XXII

The Battle of Elma

GENERAL DRU had many spies in the enemies' camp, and some of these succeeded in crossing the lines each night in order to give him what information they had been able to gather.

Some of these spies passed through the lines as late as eleven o'clock the night before the battle, and from them he learned that a general attack was to be made upon him the next day at six o'clock in the morning.

As far as he could gather, and from his own knowledge of the situation, it was General Newton's purpose to break his center. The reason Newton had this in mind was that he thought Dru's line was far flung, and he believed that if he could drive through the center, he could then throw each wing into confusion and bring about a crushing defeat.

As a matter of fact, Dru's line was not far flung, but he had a few troops strung out for many miles in order to deceive Newton, because he wanted him to try and break his center.

Up to this time, he had taken no one into his confidence, but at midnight, he called his division commanders to his headquarters and told them his plan of battle.

They were instructed not to impart any information to the commanders of brigades until two o'clock. The men were then to be aroused and given a hasty breakfast, after which they were to be ready to march by three o'clock.

Recent arrivals had augmented his army to approximately five hundred thousand men. General Newton had, as far as he could learn, approximately six hundred thousand, so there were more than a million of men facing one another.

Dru had a two-fold purpose in preparing at three in the morning. First, he wanted to take no chances upon General Newton's time of attack. His information as to six o'clock he thought reliable, but it might have been given out to deceive him and a much earlier engagement might be contemplated.

His other reason was that he intended to flank Newton on both wings.

It was his purpose to send, under cover of night, one hundred and twenty-five thousand men to the right of Newton and one hundred and twenty-five thousand to his left, and have them conceal themselves behind wooded hills until noon, and then to drive in on him from both sides.

He was confident that with two hundred and fifty thousand determined men, protected by the fortifications he had been able to erect, and with the ground of his own choosing, which had a considerable elevation over the valley through which Newton would have to march, he could hold his position until noon. He did not count upon actual fighting before eight o'clock, or perhaps not before nine.

Dru did not attempt to rest, but continued through the night to instruct his staff officers, and to arrange, as far as he could, for each contingency. Before two o'clock he was satisfied with the situation and felt assured of victory.

He was pleased to see the early morning hours develop a fog, for this would cover the march of his left and right wings, and they would not have to make so wide a detour in order that their movements might be concealed. It would also delay, he thought, Newton's attack.

His army was up and alert at three, and by four o'clock those that were to hold the center were in position, though he had them lie down again on their arms, so that they might get every moment of rest. Three o'clock saw the troops that were to flank the enemy already on the march.

At six-thirty his outposts reported Newton's army moving, but it was nine o'clock before they came within touch of his troops.

In the meantime, his men were resting, and he had food served them again as late as seven o'clock.

Newton attacked the center viciously at first, but making no headway and seeing that his men were being terribly decimated, he made a detour to the right, and, with cavalry, infantry and artillery, he drove Dru's troops in from the position which they were holding.

Dru recognized the threatened danger and sent heliograph messages to his right and left wings to begin their attack, though it was now only eleven o'clock. He then rode in person to the point of danger, and rallied his men to a firmer stand, upon which Newton could make no headway.

In that hell storm of lead and steel Dru sat upon his horse unmoved. With bared head and eyes aflame, with face flushed and exultant, he looked the embodiment of the terrible God of War. His presence and his disregard of danger incited his soldiers to deeds of valor that would forever be an "inspiration and a benediction" to the race from which they sprung.

Newton, seeing that his efforts were costing him too dearly, decided to withdraw his troops and rest until the next day, when he thought to attack Dru from the rear.

The ground was more advantageous there, and he felt confident he could dislodge him. When he gave the command to retreat, he was surprised to find Dru massing his troops outside his entrenchments and preparing to follow him. He slowly retreated and Dru as slowly followed. Newton wanted to get him well away from his stronghold and in the open plain, and then wheel and crush him. Dru was merely keeping within striking distance, so that when his two divisions got in touch with Newton they would be able to attack him on three sides.

Just as Newton was about to turn, Dru's two divisions poured down the slopes of the hills on both sides and began to charge. And when Dru's center began to charge, it was only a matter of moments before Newton's army was in a panic.

He tried to rally them and to face the on-coming enemy, but his efforts were in vain. His men threw down their guns, some surrendering, but most of them fleeing in the only way open, that towards the rear and the Lake.

Dru's soldiers saw that victory was theirs, and, maddened by the lust of war, they drove the Government forces back, killing and crushing the seething and helpless mass that was now in hopeless confusion.

Orders were given by General Dru to push on and follow the enemy until nightfall, or until the Lake was reached, where they must surrender or drown.

By six o'clock of that fateful day, the splendid army of Newton was a thing for pity, for Dru had determined to exhaust the last drop of strength of his men to make the victory complete, and the battle conclusive.

At the same time, as far as he was able, he restrained his men from killing, for he saw that the enemy were without arms, and thinking only of escape. His order was only partially obeyed, for when man is in conflict with either beast or fellowman, the primitive lust for blood comes to the fore, and the gentlest and most humane are oftentimes the most bloodthirsty.

Of the enemy forty thousand were dead and two hundred and ten thousand were wounded with seventy-five thousand missing. Of prisoners Dru had captured three hundred and seventy-five thousand.

General Newton was killed in the early afternoon, soon after the rout began.

Philip's casualties were twenty-three thousand dead and one hundred and ten thousand wounded.

It was a holocaust, but the war was indeed ended.

CHAPTER XXIII

Elma's Aftermath

AFTER General Dru had given orders for the care of the wounded and the disposition of the prisoners, he dismissed his staff and went quietly out into the starlight. He walked among the dead and wounded and saw that everything possible was being done to alleviate suffering. Feeling weary he sat for a moment upon a dismembered gun.

As he looked over the field of carnage and saw what havoc the day had made, he thought of the Selwyns and the Thors, whose selfishness and greed were responsible for it all, and he knew that they and their kind would have to meet an awful charge before the judgment seat of God. Within touch of him lay a boy of not more than seventeen, with his white face turned toward the stars. One arm was shattered and a piece of shell had torn a great red wound in the side of his chest. Dru thought him dead, but he saw him move and open his eyes. He removed a coat from a soldier that lay dead beside him and pillowed the boy's head upon it, and gave him some water and a little brandy.

"I am all in, Captain," said he, "but I would like a message sent home." He saw that Dru was an officer but he had no idea who he was. "I only enlisted last week. I live in Pennsylvania not far from here." Then more faintly— "My mother tried to persuade me to remain at home, but I wanted to do my share, so here I am—as you find me. Tell her—tell her," but the message never came—for he was dead.

After he had covered the pain-racked, ghastly face, Dru sat in silent meditation, and thought of the shame of it, the pity of it all. Somewhere amongst that human wreckage he knew

Gloria was doing what she could to comfort the wounded and those that were in the agony of death.

She had joined the Red Cross Corps of the insurgent army at the beginning of hostilities, but Dru had had only occasional glimpses of her. He was wondering now, in what part of that black and bloody field she was. His was the strong hand that had torn into fragments these helpless creatures; hers was the gentle hand that was softening the horror, the misery of it all. Dru knew there were those who felt that the result would never be worth the cost and that he, too, would come in for a measurable share of their censure. But deep and lasting as his sympathy was for those who had been brought into this maelstrom of war, yet, pessimism found no lodgment within him, rather was his great soul illuminated with the thought that with splendid heroism they had died in order that others might live the better. Twice before had the great republic been baptized in blood and each time the result had changed the thought and destiny of man. And so would it be now, only to greater purpose. Never again would the Selwyns and the Thors be able to fetter the people.

Free and unrestrained by barriers erected by the powerful, for selfish purposes, there would now lie open to them a glorious and contented future. He had it in his thoughts to do the work well now that it had been begun, and to permit no misplaced sentiment to deter him. He knew that in order to do what he had in mind, he would have to reckon with the habits and traditions of centuries, but, seeing clearly the task before him he must needs become an iconoclast and accept the consequences. For two days and nights he had been without sleep and under a physical and mental strain that would have meant disaster to any, save Philip Dru. But now he began to feel the need of rest and sleep, so he walked slowly back to his tent.

After giving orders that he was not to be disturbed, he threw himself as he was upon his camp bed, and, oblivious of the fact that the news of his momentous victory had circled the globe and that his name was upon the lips of half the world, he fell into a dreamless, restful sleep.

CHAPTER XXIV

Uncrowned Heroes

WHEN Dru wakened in the morning after a long and refreshing sleep, his first thoughts were of Gloria Strawn. Before leaving his tent he wrote her an invitation to dine with him that evening in company with some of his generals and their wives. All through that busy day Dru found himself looking forward to the coming evening. When Gloria came Dru was standing at the door of his tent to meet her. As he helped her from the army conveyance she said:

"Oh, Philip, how glad I am! How glad I am!"

Dru knew that she had no reference to his brilliant victory, but that it was his personal welfare that she had in mind.

During the dinner many stories of heroism were told, men who were least suspected of great personal bravery had surprised their comrades by deeds that would follow the coming centuries in both song and story. Dru, who had been a silent listener until now, said:

"Whenever my brother soldier rises above self and gives or offers his life for that of his comrade, no one rejoices more than I. But, my friends, the highest courage is not displayed upon the battlefield. The soldier's heroism is done under stress of great excitement, and his field of action is one that appeals to the imagination. It usually also touches our patriotism and self-esteem. The real heroes of the world are oftentimes never known. I once knew a man of culture and wealth who owned a plantation in some hot and inaccessible region. Smallpox in its most virulent form became prevalent among the negroes. Everyone fled the place save this man, and those that were stricken. Single-handed and alone, he nursed them while they lived and buried them when they died. And yet during all the years I knew him, never once did he refer to it. An old negro told me the story and others afterwards confirmed it. This same man jumped into a swollen river and rescued a poor old negro who could not swim. There was no one to applaud him as he battled with the deadly eddies and currents and brought to safety one of the least of God's creatures. To my mind the flag of no nation ever waved above a braver, nobler heart."

There was a moment's silence, and then Gloria said:

"Philip, the man you mention is doubtless the most splendid product of our civilization, for he was perhaps as gentle as he was brave, but there is still another type of hero to whom I would call attention. I shall tell you of a man named Sutton, whom I came to know in my settlement work and who seemed to those who knew him wholly bad. He was cruel, selfish, and without any sense of honor, and even his personality was repulsive, and yet this is what he did.

"One day, soon after dark, the ten story tenement building in which he lived caught fire. Smoke was pouring from the windows, at which many frightened faces were seen.

"But what was holding the crowd's breathless attention, was the daring attempt of a man on the eighth floor to save a child of some five or six years.

"He had gotten from his room to a small iron balcony, and there he took his handkerchief and blindfolded the little boy. He lifted the child over the railing, and let him down to a stone ledge some twelve inches wide, and which seemed to be five or six feet below the balcony.

"The man had evidently told the child to flatten himself against the wall, for the little fellow had spread out his arms and pressed his body close to it.

"When the man reached him, he edged him along in front of

him. It was a perilous journey, and to what end?

"No one could see that he was bettering his condition by moving further along the building, though it was evident he had a well-defined purpose from the beginning.

"When he reached the corner, he stopped in front of a large flagpole that projected out from the building some twenty or more feet.

"He shouted to the firemen in the street below, but his voice was lost in the noise and distance. He then scribbled something on an envelope and after wrapping his knife inside, dropped it down. He lost no time by seeing whether he was understood, but he took the child and put his arms and legs about the pole in front of him and together they slid along to the golden ball at the end.

"What splendid courage! What perfect self-possession! He then took the boy's arm above the hand and swung him clear. He held him for a moment to see that all was ready below, and turned him loose.

"The child dropped as straight as a plummet into the canvas net that was being held for him.

"The excitement had been so tense up to now, that in all that vast crowd no one said a word or moved a muscle, but when they saw the little fellow unhurt, and perched high on the shoulders of a burly fireman, such cheers were given as were never before heard in that part of New York.

"The man, it seemed, knew as well as those below, that his weight made impossible his escape in a like manner, for he had slid back to the building and was sitting upon the ledge smoking a cigarette.

"At first it was the child in which the crowd was interested, but now it was the man. He must be saved; but could he be? The heat was evidently becoming unbearable and from time to time a smother of smoke hid him from view. Once when it cleared away he was no longer there, it had suffocated him and he had fallen, a mangled heap, into the street below.

"That man was Sutton, and the child was not his own. He could have saved himself had he not stayed to break in a door behind which the screams of the child were heard."

There was a long silence when Gloria had ended her story, and then the conversation ran along more cheerful lines.

CHAPTER XXV

The Administrator of the Republic

GENERAL DRU began at once the reorganization of his army. The Nation knew that the war was over, and it was in a quiver of excitement.

They recognized the fact that Dru dominated the situation and that a master mind had at last arisen in the Republic. He had a large and devoted army to do his bidding, and the future seemed to lie wholly in his hands.

The great metropolitan dailies were in keen rivalry to obtain some statement from him, but they could not get within speaking distance. The best they could do was to fill their columns with speculations and opinions from those near, or at least pretending to be near him. He had too much to do to waste a moment, but he had it in mind to make some statement of a general nature within a few days.

The wounded were cared for, the dead disposed of and all prisoners disarmed and permitted to go to their homes under parole. Of his own men he relieved those who had sickness in their families, or pressing duties to perform. Many of the prisoners, at their urgent solicitation, he enlisted. The final result was a compact and fairly well organized army of some four hundred thousand men who were willing to serve as long as they were needed.

During the days that Dru was reorganizing, he now and then saw Gloria. She often wondered why Philip did not tell her something of his plans, and at times she felt hurt at his reticence. She did not know that he would have trusted her with his life without hesitation, but that his sense of duty sealed his lips when it came to matters of public policy.

119

He knew she would not willingly betray him, but he never took chances upon the judgment she, or any friend, might exercise as to what was or what was not important. When a thought or plan had once gone from him to another it was at the mercy of the other's discretion, and good intention did not avail if discretion and judgment were lacking. He consulted freely with those from whom he thought he could obtain help, but about important matters no one ever knew but himself his conclusions.

Dru was now ready to march upon Washington, and he issued an address to his soldiers which was intended, in fact, for the general public. He did not want, at this time, to assume unusual powers, and if he had spoken to the Nation he might be criticised as assuming a dictatorial attitude.

He complimented his army upon their patriotism and upon their bravery, and told them that they had won what was, perhaps, the most important victory in the history of warfare. He deplored the fact that, of necessity, it was a victory over their fellow countrymen, but he promised that the breach would soon be healed, for it was his purpose to treat them as brothers. He announced that no one, neither the highest nor the lowest, would be arrested, tried, or in any way disturbed provided they accepted the result of the battle as final, and as determining a change in the policy of government in accordance with the views held by those whom he represented. Failure to acquiesce in this, or any attempt to foster the policies of the *late government,* would be considered seditious, and would be punished by death. He was determined upon immediate peace and quietude, and any individual, newspaper or corporation violating this order would be summarily dealt with.

The words "late government" caused a sensation. It pointed very surely to the fact that as soon as Dru reached Washington, he would assume charge of affairs. But in what way? That was the momentous question.

President Rockwell, the Vice-President and the Cabinet, fearful of the result of Dru's complete domination, fled the country. Selwyn urged, threatened, and did all he could to have them stand their ground, and take the consequences of defeat, but to no avail. Finally, he had the Secretary of State resign, so that the President might appoint him to that office. This being done, he became acting President.

There were some fifty thousand troops at Washington and vicinity, and Dru wired Selwyn asking whether any defense of that city was contemplated. Upon receiving a negative answer, he sent one of his staff officers directly to Washington to demand a formal surrender. Selwyn acquiesced in this, and while the troops were not disbanded, they were placed under the command of Dru's emissary.

After further negotiations it was arranged for such of the volunteers as desired to do so, to return to their homes. This left a force of thirty thousand men at Washington who accepted the new conditions, and declared fealty to Dru and the cause he represented. There was now requisitioned all the cars that were necessary to convey the army from Buffalo to New York, Philadelphia and Washington. A day was named when all other traffic was to be stopped, until the troops, equipment and supplies had been conveyed to their destinations. One hundred thousand men were sent to New York and one hundred thousand to Philadelphia, and held on the outskirts of those cities. Two hundred thousand were sent to Washington and there Dru went himself.

Selwyn made a formal surrender to him and was placed under arrest, but it was hardly more than a formality, for Selwyn was placed under no further restraint than that he should not leave Washington. His arrest was made for its effect upon the Nation; in order to make it clear that the former government no longer existed.

General Dru now called a conference of his officers and announced his purpose of assuming the powers of a dictator, distasteful as it was to him, and, as he felt it might also be, to the people. He explained that such a radical step was necessary, in order to quickly purge the Government of those abuses that had arisen, and give to it the form and purpose for which they had fought. They were assured that he was free from any personal ambition, and he pledged his honor to retire after the contemplated reforms had been made, so that the country could again have a constitutional government. Not one of them doubted his word, and they pledged themselves and the men under them, to sustain him loyally. He then issued an address to his army proclaiming himself "*Administrator of the Republic.*"

CHAPTER XXVI

Dru Outlines His Intentions

THE day after this address was issued, General Dru reviewed his army and received such an ovation that it stilled criticism, for it was plain that the new order of things had to be accepted, and there was a thrill of fear among those who would have liked to raise their voices in protest.

It was felt that the property and lives of all were now in the keeping of one man.

Dru's first official act was to call a conference of those, throughout the Union, who had been leaders in the movement to overthrow the Government.

The gathering was large and representative, but he found no such unanimity as amongst the army. A large part, perhaps a majority, were outspoken for an immediate return to representative government.

They were willing that unusual powers should be assumed long enough to declare the old Government illegal, and to issue an immediate call for a general election, state and national, to be held as usual in November. The advocates of this plan were willing that Dru should remain in authority until the duly constituted officials could be legally installed.

Dru presided over the meeting, therefore he took no part in the early discussion, further than to ask for the fullest expression of opinion. After hearing the plan for a limited dictatorship proposed, he arose, and, in a voice vibrant with emotion, addressed the meeting as follows:

"My fellow countrymen:—I feel sure that however much we may differ as to methods, there is no one within the sound of my voice that does not wish me well, and none, I believe, mistrusts either my honesty of purpose, my patriotism, or my ultimate desire to restore as soon as possible to our distracted land a constitutional government.

"We all agreed that a change had to be brought about even though it meant revolution, for otherwise the cruel hand of avarice would have crushed out from us, and from our children, every semblance of freedom. If our late masters had been more moderate in their greed we would have been content to struggle for yet another period, hoping that in time we might again have justice and equality before the law. But even so we would have had a defective Government, defective in machinery and defective in its constitution and laws. To have righted it, a century of public education would have been necessary. The present opportunity has been bought at fearful cost. If we use it lightly, those who fell upon the field of Elma will have died in vain, and the anguish of mothers, and the tears of widows and orphans will mock us because we failed in our duty to their beloved dead.

"For a long time I have known that this hour would come, and that there would be those of you who would stand affrighted at the momentous change from constitutional government to despotism, no matter how pure and exalted you might believe my intentions to be.

"But in the long watches of the night, in the solitude of my tent, I conceived a plan of government which, by the grace of God, I hope to be able to give to the American people. My life is consecrated to our cause, and, hateful as is the thought of assuming supreme power, I can see no other way clearly, and I would be recreant to my trust if I faltered in my duty. Therefore, with the aid I know each one of you will give me, there shall, in God's good time, be wrought 'a government of the people, by the people and for the people.'"

When Dru had finished there was generous applause. At first here and there a dissenting voice was heard, but the chorus of approval drowned it.

It was a splendid tribute to his popularity and integrity. When quiet was restored, he named twelve men whom he wanted to take charge of the departments and to act as his advisors.

They were all able men, each distinguished in his own field of endeavor, and when their names were announced there was an outburst of satisfaction.

The meeting adjourned, and each member went home a believer in Dru and the policy he had adopted. They, in turn, converted the people to their view of the situation, so that Dru was able to go forward with his great work, conscious of the support and approval of an overwhelming majority of his fellow countrymen.

CHAPTER XXVII

A New Era at Washington

WHEN General Dru assumed the responsibilities of Government he saw that, unless he arranged it otherwise, social duties would prove a tax upon his time and would deter him from working with that celerity for which he had already become famous. He had placed Mr. Strawn at the head of the Treasury Department and he offered him the use of the White House as a place of residence. His purpose was to have Mrs. Strawn and Gloria relieve him of those social functions that are imposed upon the heads of all Governments. Mrs. Strawn was delighted with such an arrangement, and it almost compensated her for having been forced by her husband and Gloria into the ranks of the popular or insurgent party. Dru continued to use the barracks as his home, though he occupied the offices in the White House for public business. It soon became a familiar sight in Washington to see him ride swiftly through the streets on his seal-brown gelding, Twilight, as he went to and from the barracks and the White House. Dru gave and attended dinners to foreign ambassadors and special envoys, but at the usual entertainments given to the public or to the official family he was seldom seen. He and Gloria were in accord, regarding the character of entertainments to be given, and all unnecessary display was to be avoided. This struck a cruel blow at Mrs. Strawn, who desired to have everything in as sumptuous a way as under the old régime, but both Dru and Gloria were as adamant, and she had to be content with the new order of things.

"Gloria," said Dru, "It pleases me beyond measure to find ourselves so nearly in accord concerning the essential things, and I am glad to believe that you express your convictions candidly and are not merely trying to please me."

"That, Philip, is because we are largely striving for the same purposes. We both want, I think, to take the selfish equation out of our social fabric. We want to take away the sting from poverty, and we want envy to have no place in the world of our making. Is it not so?"

"That seems to me, Gloria, to be the crux of our endeavors. But when we speak of unselfishness, as we now have it in mind, we are entering a hitherto unknown realm. The definition of selfishness yesterday or to-day is quite another thing from the unselfishness that we have in view, and which we hope and expect will soon leaven society. I think, perhaps, we may reach the result quicker if we call it mankind's new and higher pleasure or happiness, for that is what it will mean."

"Philip, it all seems too altruistic ever to come in our lifetime; but, do you know, I am awfully optimistic about it. I really believe it will come so quickly, after it once gets a good start, that it will astound us. The proverbial snowball coming down the mountain side will be as nothing to it. Everyone will want to join the procession at once. No one will want to be left out for the finger of Scorn to accuse. And, strangely enough, I believe it will be the educated and rich, in fact the ones that are now the most selfish, that will be in the vanguard of the procession. They will be the first to realize the joy of it all, and in this way will they redeem the sins of their ancestors."

"Your enthusiasm, Gloria, readily imparts itself to me, and my heart quickens with hope that what you say may be prophetic. But, to return to the immediate work in hand, let us simplify our habits and customs to as great a degree as is possible under existing circumstances. One of the causes for the mad rush for money is the desire to excel our friends and neighbors in our manner of living, our entertainments and the like. Everyone has been trying to keep up with the most extravagant of his set: the result must, in the end, be unhappiness for all and disaster for many. What a pitiful ambition it is! How soul-lowering! How it narrows the horizon! We cannot help the poor, we cannot aid our neighbor, for, if we do, we cannot keep our places in the unholy struggle for social equality within our little sphere. Let us go, Gloria, into the fresh air, for it stifles me to think of this phase of our civilization. I wish I had let our discussion remain upon the high peak where you placed it and from which we gazed into the promised land."

CHAPTER XXVIII

An International Crisis

THE Administrator did nothing towards reducing the army which, including those in the Philippines and elsewhere, totaled five hundred thousand. He thought this hardly sufficient considering international conditions, and one of his first acts was to increase the number of men to six hundred thousand and to arm and equip them thoroughly.

For a long period of years England had maintained relations with the United States that amounted to an active alliance, but there was evidence that she had under discussion, with her old-time enemy, Germany, a treaty by which that nation was to be allowed a free hand in South America.

In return for this England was to be conceded all German territory in Africa, and was to be allowed to absorb, eventually, that entire continent excepting that part belonging to France.

Japan, it seemed, was to be taken into the agreement and was to be given her will in the East. If she desired the Philippines, she might take them as far as European interference went. Her navy was more powerful than any the United States could readily muster in the far Pacific, and England would, if necessary, serve notice upon us that her gunboats were at Japan's disposal in case of war.

In return, Japan was to help in maintaining British supremacy in India, which was now threatened by the vigorous young Republic of China.

The latter nation did not wish to absorb India herself, but she was committed to the policy of "Asia for the Asiatics," and it did not take much discernment to see that some day soon this would come about.

China and Japan had already reached an agreement concerning certain matters of interest between them, the most important being that Japan should maintain a navy twice as powerful as that of China, and that the latter should have an army one-third more powerful than that of Japan. The latter was to confine her sphere of influence to the Islands of the Sea and to Korea, and, in the event of a combined attack on Russia, which was contemplated, they were to acquire Siberia as far west as practicable, and divide that territory. China had already by purchase, concessions and covert threats, regained that part of her territory once held by England, Germany and France. She had a powerful army and a navy of some consequence, therefore she must needs to be reckoned with.

England's hold upon Canada was merely nominal, therefore, further than as a matter of pride, it was of slight importance to her whether she lost it or not. Up to the time of the revolution, Canada had been a hostage, and England felt that she could at no time afford a rupture with us. But the alluring vision that Germany held out to her was dazzling her statesmen. Africa all red from the Cape to the Mediterranean and from Madagascar to the Atlantic was most alluring. And it seemed so easy of accomplishment. Germany maintained her military superiority, as England, even then, held a navy equal to any two powers.

Germany was to exploit South America without reference to the Monroe Doctrine, and England was to give her moral support, and the support of her navy, if necessary. If the United States objected to the extent of declaring war, they were prepared to meet that issue. Together, they could put into commission a navy three times as strong as that of the United States, and with Canada as a base, and with a merchant marine fifty times as large as that of the United States, they could convey half a million men to North America as quickly as Dru could send a like number to San Francisco. If Japan joined the movement, she could occupy the Pacific Slope as long as England and Germany were her allies.

The situation which had sprung up while the United States was putting her own house in order, was full of peril and General Dru gave it his careful and immediate attention.

None of the powers at interest knew that Dru's Government had the slightest intimation of what was being discussed. The information had leaked through one of the leading international banking houses, that had been approached concerning a possible loan for a very large amount, and the secret had reached Selwyn through Thor.

Selwyn not only gave General Dru this information, but much else that was of extreme value. Dru soon came to know that at heart Selwyn was not without patriotism, and that it was only from environment and an overweening desire for power that had led him into the paths he had heretofore followed.

Selwyn would have preferred ruling through the people rather than through the interests and the machinations of corrupt politics, but he had little confidence that the people would take enough interest in public affairs to make this possible, and to deviate from the path he had chosen, meant, he thought, disaster to his ambitions.

Dru's career proved him wrong, and no one was quicker to see it than Selwyn. Dru's remarkable insight into character fathomed the real man, and, in a cautious and limited way, he counseled with him as the need arose.

CHAPTER XXIX

The Reform of the Judiciary

OF HIS Council of Twelve, the Administrator placed one member in charge of each of the nine departments, and gave to the other three special work that was constantly arising.

One of his advisers was a man of distinguished lineage, but who, in his early youth, had been compelled to struggle against those unhappy conditions that followed reconstruction in the South. His intellect and force of character had brought him success in his early manhood, and he was the masterful head of a university that, under his guidance, was soon to become one of the foremost in the world. He was a trained political economist, and had rare discernment in pubic affairs, therefore Dru leaned heavily upon him when he began to rehabilitate the Government.

Dru used Selwyn's unusual talents for organization and administration, in thoroughly overhauling the actual machinery of both Federal and State Governments. There was no doubt but that there was an enormous waste going on, and this he undertook to stop, for he felt sure that as much efficiency could be obtained at two-thirds the cost. One of his first acts as Administrator was to call together five great lawyers, who had no objectionable corporate or private practice, and give to them the task of defining the powers of all courts, both State and Federal.

They were not only to remodel court procedure, but to eliminate such courts as were unnecessary. To this board he gave the further task of reconstructing the rules governing lawyers, their practice before the courts, their relations to their clients and the amount and character of their fees under given condi-

135

tions.

Under Dru's instruction the commission was to limit the power of the courts to the extent that they could no longer pass upon the constitutionality of laws, their function being merely to decide, as between litigants, what the law was, as was the practice of all other civilized nations.

Judges, both Federal and State, were to be appointed for life, subject to compulsory retirement at seventy, and to forced retirement at any time by a two-thirds vote of the House and a majority vote of the Senate. Their appointment was to be suggested by the President or Governor, as the case might be, and a majority vote of the House and a two-third vote of the Senate were necessary for confirmation.

High salaries were to be paid, but the number of judges was to be largely decreased, perhaps by two-thirds. This would be possible, because the simplification of procedure and the curtailment of their powers would enormously lessen the amount of work to be done. Dru called the Board's attention to the fact that England had about two hundred judges of all kinds, while there were some thirty-six hundred in the United States, and that the reversals by the English Courts were only about three per cent. of the reversals by the American Courts.

The United States had, therefore, the most complicated, expensive and inadequate legal machinery of any civilized nation. Lawyers were no longer to be permitted to bring suits of doubtful character, and without facts and merit to sustain them. Hereafter it would be necessary for the attorney, and the client himself, to swear to the truth of the allegations submitted in their petitions of suits and briefs.

If they could not show that they had good reason to believe that their cause was just, they would be subject to fines and imprisonment, besides being subject to damages by the defendant. Dru desired the Board on Legal Procedure and Judiciary to work out a fair and comprehensive system, based along the fundamental lines he had laid down, so that the people might be no longer ridden by either the law or the lawyer. It was his intention that no man was to be suggested for a judgeship or confirmed who was known to drink to excess, either regularly or periodically, or one who was known not to pay his personal debts, or had acted in a reprehensible manner either in private or in his public capacity as a lawyer.

Any of these habits or actions occurring after appointment was to subject him to impeachment. Moreover, any judge who used his position to favor any individual or corporation, or who deviated from the path of even and exact justice for all, or who heckled a litigant, witness or attorney, or who treated them in an unnecessarily harsh or insulting manner, was to be, upon complaint duly attested to by reliable witnesses, tried for impeachment.

The Administrator was positive in his determination to have the judiciary a most efficient bureau of the people, and to have it sufficiently well paid to obtain the best talent. He wanted it held in the highest esteem, and to have an appointment thereon considered one of the greatest honors of the Republic. To do this he knew it was necessary for its members to be able, honest, temperate and considerate.

Chapter XXX

A New Code of Laws

Dru selected another board of five lawyers, and to them he gave the task of reforming legal procedure and of pruning down the existing laws, both State and National, cutting out the obsolete and useless ones and rewriting those recommended to be retained, in plain and direct language free from useless legal verbiage and understandable to the ordinary lay citizen.

He then created another board, of even greater ability, to read, digest and criticize the work of the other two boards and report their findings directly to him, giving a brief summary of their reasons and recommendations. To assist in this work he engaged in an advisory capacity three eminent lawyers from England, Germany and France respectively.

The three boards were urged to proceed with as much despatch as possible, for Dru knew that it would take at least several years to do it properly, and afterwards he would want to place the new code of laws in working order under the reformed judiciary before he would be content to retire. The other changes he had in mind he thought could be accomplished much more quickly.

Among other things, Dru directed that the States should have a simplification of land titles, so that transfers of real estate could be made as easy as the transfer of stocks, and with as little expense, no attorneys' fees for examination of titles, and no recording fees being necessary. The title could not be contested after being once registered in a name, therefore no litigation over real property could be possible. It was estimated by Dru's statisticians that in some States this would save the people annually a sum equal to the cost of running their governments.

A uniform divorce law was also to be drawn and put into operation, so that the scandals arising from the old conditions might no longer be possible.

It was arranged that when laws affecting the States had been written, before they went into effect they were to be submitted to a body of lawyers made up of one representative from each State. This body could make suggestions for such additions or eliminations as might seem to them pertinent, and conforming with conditions existing in their respective commonwealths, but the board was to use its judgment in the matter of incorporating the suggestions in the final draft of the law. It was not the Administrator's purpose to rewrite at that time the Federal and State Constitutions, but to do so at a later date when the laws had been rewritten and decided upon; he wished to first satisfy himself as to them and their adaptability to the existing conditions, and then make a constitution conforming with them. This would seem to be going at things backward, but it recommended itself to Dru as the sane and practical way to have the constitutions and laws in complete harmony.

The formation of the three boards created much disturbance among judges, lawyers and corporations, but when the murmur began to assume the proportions of a loud-voiced protest, General Dru took the matter in hand. He let it be known that it would be well for them to cease to foment trouble. He pointed out that heretofore the laws had been made for the judges, for the lawyers and for those whose financial or political influence enabled them to obtain special privileges, but that hereafter the whole legal machinery was to be run absolutely in the interest of the people. The decisive and courageous manner in which he handled this situation, brought him the warm and generous approval of the people and they felt that at last their day had come.

CHAPTER XXXI

The Question of Taxation

THE question of taxation was one of the most complex problems with which the Administrator had to deal. As with the legal machinery he formed a board of five to advise with him, and to carry out his very well-defined ideas. Upon this board was a political economist, a banker, who was thought to be the ablest man of his profession, a farmer who was a very successful and practical man, a manufacturer and a Congressman, who for many years had been the consequential member of the Ways and Means Committee. All these men were known for their breadth of view and their interest in public affairs.

Again, Dru went to England, France and Germany for the best men he could get as advisers to the Board. He offered such a price for their services that, eminent as they were, they did not feel that they could refuse. He knew the best were the cheapest.

At the first sitting of the Committee, Dru told them to consider every existing tax law obliterated, to begin anew and to construct a revenue system along the lines he indicated for municipalities, counties, states and the Nation. He did not contemplate, he said, that the new law should embrace all the taxes which the three first-named civil divisions could levy, but that it should apply only where taxes related to the general government. Nevertheless, Dru was hopeful that such a system would be devised as would render it unnecessary for either municipalities, counties or states to require any further revenue. Dru directed the board to divide each state into districts for the purpose of taxation, not making them large enough to be cumbersome, and yet not small enough to prohibit the employment of able men to form the assessment and collecting boards. He suggested that these boards be composed of four local men and one representative of the Nation.

He further directed that the tax on realty both in the country and the city should be upon the following basis: — Improvements on city property were to be taxed at one-fifth of their value, and the naked property either in town or country at two-thirds of its value. The fact that country property used for agricultural purposes was improved, should not be reckoned. In other words, if A had one hundred acres with eighty acres of it in cultivation and otherwise improved, and B had one hundred acres beside him of just as good land, but not in cultivation or improved, B's land should be taxed as much as A's.

In cities and towns taxation was to be upon a similar basis. For instance, when there was a lot, say, one hundred feet by one hundred feet with improvements upon it worth three hundred thousand dollars, and there was another lot of the same size and value, the improved lot should be taxed only sixty thousand more than the unimproved lot; that is, both lots should be taxed alike, and the improvement on the one should be assessed at sixty thousand dollars or one-fifth of its actual value.

This, Dru pointed out, would deter owners from holding unimproved realty, for the purpose of getting the unearned increment made possible by the thrift of their neighbors. In the country it would open up land for cultivation now lying idle, provide homes for more people, cheapen the cost of living to all, and make possible better schools, better roads and a better opportunity for the successful cooperative marketing of products.

In the cities and towns, it would mean a more homogenous population, with better streets, better sidewalks, better sewerage, more convenient churches and cheaper rents and homes. As it was at that time, a poor man could not buy a home nor rent one near his work, but must needs go to the outskirts of his town, necessitating loss of time and cost of transportation, besides sacrificing the obvious comforts and conveniences of a more compact population.

The Administrator further directed the tax board to work out a graduated income tax exempting no income whatsoever. Incomes up to one thousand dollars a year, Dru thought, should bear a merely nominal tax of one-half of one per cent.; those of from one to two thousand, one per cent.; those of from two to five thousand, two per cent.; those of from five to ten thousand, three per cent.; those of from ten to twenty thousand, six per cent. The tax on incomes of more than twenty thousand dollars a year, Dru directed, was to be rapidly increased, until a maximum of seventy per cent was to be reached on those incomes that were ten million dollars, or above.

False returns, false swearing, or any subterfuge to defraud the Government, was to be punished by not less than six months or more than two years in prison. The board was further instructed to incorporate in their tax measure, an inheritance tax clause, graduated at the same rate as in the income tax, and to safeguard the defrauding of the Government by gifts before death and other devices.

CHAPTER XXXII

A Federal Incorporation Act

ALONG with the first board on tax laws, Administrator Dru appointed yet another commission to deal with another phase of this subject. The second board was composed of economists and others well versed in matters relating to the tariff and Internal Revenue, who, broadly speaking, were instructed to work out a tariff law which would contemplate the abolishment of the theory of protection as a governmental policy. A tariff was to be imposed mainly as a supplement to the other taxes, the revenue from which, it was thought, would be almost sufficient for the needs of the Government, considering the economies that were being made.

Dru's father had been an ardent advocate of State rights, and the Administrator had been reared in that atmosphere; but when he began to think out such questions for himself, he realized that density of population and rapid inter-communication afforded by electric and steam railroads, motors, aeroplanes, telegraphs and telephones were, to all practical purposes, obliterating State lines and molding the country into a homogeneous nation.

Therefore, after the Revolution, Dru saw that the time had come for this trend to assume more definite form, and for the National Government to take upon itself some of the functions heretofore exclusively within the jurisdiction of the States. Up to the time of the Revolution a state of chaos had existed. For instance, laws relating to divorces, franchises, interstate commerce, sanitation and many other things were different in each State, and nearly all were inefficient and not conducive to the general welfare. Administrator Dru therefore concluded that the time had come when a measure of control of such things should be vested in the Central Government. He therefore proposed enacting into the general laws a Federal Incorporation Act, and into his scheme of taxation a franchise tax that would not be more burdensome than that now imposed by the States. He also proposed making corporations share with the Government and States a certain part of their net earnings, public service corporations to a greater extent than others. Dru's plan contemplated that either the Government or the State in which the home or headquarters of any corporation was located was to have representation upon the boards of such corporation, in order that the interests of the National, State, or City Government could be protected, and so as to insure publicity in the event it was needful to correct abuses.

He had incorporated in the Franchise Law the right of Labor to have one representative upon the boards of corporations and to share a certain percentage of the earnings above their wages, after a reasonable per cent upon the capital had been earned.[1] In turn, it was to be obligatory upon them not to strike, but to submit all grievances to arbitration. The law was to stipulate that if the business prospered, wages should be high; if times were dull, they should be reduced.

The people were asked to curb their prejudice against corporations. It was promised that in the future corporations should be honestly run, and in the interest of the stockholders and the public. Dru expressed the hope that their formation would be welcomed rather than discouraged, for he was sure that under the new law it would be more to the public advantage to have business conducted by corporations than by individuals in a private capacity. In the taxation of real estate, the unfair practice of taxing it at full value when mortgaged and then taxing

[1] See page 241

the holder of the mortgage, was to be abolished. The same was to be true of bonded indebtedness on any kind of property. The easy way to do this was to tax property and not tax the evidence of debt, but Dru preferred the other method, that of taxing the property, less the debt, and then taxing the debt wherever found.

His reason for this was that, if bonds or other forms of debt paid no taxes, it would have a tendency to make investors put money into that kind of security, even though the interest was correspondingly low, in order to avoid the trouble of rendering and paying taxes on them. This, he thought, might keep capital out of other needful enterprises, and give a glut of money in one direction and a paucity in another. Money itself was not to be taxed as was then done in so many States.

CHAPTER XXXIII

The Railroad Problem

WHILE the boards and commissions appointed by Administrator Dru were working out new tax, tariff and revenue laws, establishing the judiciary and legal machinery on a new basis and revising the general law, it was necessary that the financial system of the country also should be reformed. Dru and his advisers saw the difficulties of attacking this most intricate question, but with the advice and assistance of a commission appointed for that purpose, they began the formulation of a new banking law, affording a flexible currency, bottomed largely upon commercial assets, the real wealth of the nation, instead of upon debt, as formerly.

This measure was based upon the English, French and German plans, its authors taking the best from each and making the whole conform to American needs and conditions. Dru regarded this as one of his most pressing reforms, for he hoped that it would not only prevent panics, as formerly, but that its final construction would completely destroy the credit trust, the greatest, the most far reaching and, under evil direction, the most pernicious trust of all.

While in this connection, as well as all others, he was insistent that business should be honestly conducted, yet it was his purpose to throw all possible safeguards around it. In the past it had been not only harassed by a monetary system that was a mere patchwork affair and entirely inadequate to the needs of the times, but it had been constantly threatened by tariff, railroad and other legislation calculated to cause continued disturbance. The ever-present demagogue had added to the confusion, and, altogether, legitimate business had suffered more during the long season of unrest than had the law-defying monopolies.

Dru wanted to see the nation prosper, as he knew it could never have done that under the old order, where the few reaped a disproportionate reward and to this end he spared no pains in perfecting the new financial system. In the past the railroads and a few industrial monopolies had come in for the greatest amount of abuse and prejudice. This feeling while largely just, in his opinion, had done much harm. The railroads were the offenders in the first instance, he knew, and then the people retaliated, and in the end both the capitalists who actually furnished the money to build the roads and the people suffered.

"In the first place," said Administrator Dru to his counsel during the discussion of the new financial system, "the roads were built dishonestly. Money was made out of their construction by the promoters in the most open and shameless way, and afterwards bonds and stocks were issued far in excess of the fraudulent so-called cost. Nor did the iniquity end there. Enterprises were started, some of a public nature such as grain elevators and cotton compresses, in which the officials of the railroads were financially interested. These favored concerns received rebates and better shipping facilities than their competitors and competition was stifled.

"Iron mines and mills, lumber mills and yards, coal mines and yards, etc., etc., went into their rapacious maw, and the managers considered the railroads a private snap and 'the public be damned.'

"These things," continued Dru, "did not constitute their sole offense, for, as you all know, they lobbied through legislatures the most unconscionable bills, giving them land, money and rights to further exploit the public.

"But the thing that, perhaps, aroused resentment most was

their failure to pay just claims. The idea in the old days, as you remember, was to pay nothing, and make it so expensive to litigate that one would prefer to suffer an injustice rather than go to court. From this policy was born the claim lawyer, who financed and fought through the courts personal injury claims, until it finally came to pass that in loss or damage suits the average jury would decide against the railroad on general principles. In such cases the litigant generally got all he claimed and the railroad was mulcted. There is no estimating how much this unfortunate policy cost the railroads of America up to the time of the Revolution. The trouble was that the ultimate loss fell, not on those who inaugurated it but upon the innocent stock and bondholder of the roads.

"While the problem is complicated," he continued, "its solution lies in the new financial system, together with the new system of control of public utilities."

To this end, Dru laid down his plans by which public service corporations should be honestly, openly and efficiently run, so that the people should have good service at a minimum cost.

Primarily the general Government, the state or the city, as the case might be, were to have representation on the directorate, as previously indicated. They were to have full access to the books, and semi-annually each corporation was to be compelled to make public a full and a clear report, giving the receipts and expenditures, including salaries paid to high officials. These corporations were also to be under the control of national and state commissions.

While the Nation and State were to share in the earnings, Dru demanded that the investor in such corporate securities should have reasonable profits, and the fullest protection, in the event states or municipalities attempted to deal unfairly with them, as had heretofore been the case in many instances.

The Administrator insisted upon the prohibition of franchise to "holding companies" of whatsoever character. In the past, he declared, they had been prolific trust breeders, and those existing at that time, he asserted, should be dissolved.

Under the new law, as Dru outlined it, one company might control another, but it would have to be with the consent of both the state and federal officials having jurisdiction in the premises, and it would have to be clear that the public would be benefited thereby. There was to be in the future no hiding under cover, for everything was to be done in the open, and in a way entirely understandable to the ordinary layman.

Certain of the public service corporations, Dru insisted, should be taken over bodily by the National Government and accordingly the Postmaster General was instructed to negotiate with the telegraph and telephone companies for their properties at a fair valuation. They were to be under the absolute control of the Post Office Department, and the people were to have the transmission of all messages at cost, just as they had their written ones. A parcel post was also inaugurated, so that as much as twelve pounds could be sent at cost.

Chapter XXXIV

Selwyn's Story

The further Administrator Dru carried his progress of reform, the more helpful he found Selwyn. Dru's generous treatment of him had brought in return a grateful loyalty.

One stormy night, after Selwyn had dined with Dru, he sat contentedly smoking by a great log fire in the library of the small cottage which Dru occupied in the barracks.

"This reminds me," he said, "of my early boyhood, and of the fireplace in the old tavern where I was born."

General Dru had long wanted to know of Selwyn, and, though they had arranged to discuss some important business, Dru urged the former Senator to tell him something of his early life.

Selwyn consented, but asked that the lights be turned off so that there would be only the glow from the fire, in order that it might seem more like the old days at home when his father's political cronies gathered about the hearth for their confidential talks.

And this was Selwyn's story:—

My father was a man of small education and kept a tavern on the outer edge of Philadelphia. I was his only child, my mother dying in my infancy.

There was a bar connected with the house, and it was a rendezvous for the politicians of our ward.

I became interested in politics so early that I cannot remember the time when I was not. My father was a temperate man, strong-willed and able, and I have often wondered since that he was content to end his days without trying to get beyond the environments of a small tavern.

He was sensitive, and perhaps his lack of education caused him to hesitate to enter a larger and more conspicuous field.

However, he was resolved that I should not be hampered as he was, and I was, therefore, given a good common school education first, and afterwards sent to Girard College, where I graduated, the youngest of my class.

Much to my father's delight, I expressed a desire to study law, for it seemed to us both that this profession held the best opportunity open to me. My real purpose in becoming a lawyer was to aid me in politics, for it was clear to both my father and me that I had an unusual aptitude therefor.

My study of law was rather cursory than real, and did not lead to a profound knowledge of the subject, but it was sufficient for me to obtain admittance to the bar, and it was not long, young as I was, before my father's influence brought me a practice that was lucrative and which required but little legal lore.

At that time the ward boss was a man by the name of Marx. While his father was a German, he was almost wholly Irish, for his father died when he was young, and he was reared by a masculine, masterful, though ignorant Irish mother.

He was my father's best friend, and there were no secrets between them. They seldom paid attention to me, and I was rarely dismissed even when they had their most confidential talks.

In this way, I early learned how our great American cities are looted, not so much by those actually in power, for they are of less consequence than the more powerful men behind them.

If any contract of importance was to be let, be it either public or private, Marx and his satellites took their toll. He, in his turn, had to account to the man above, the city boss.

If a large private undertaking was contemplated, the ward

boss had to be seen and consulted as to the best contractors, and it was understood that at least five per cent. more than the work was worth had to be paid, otherwise, there would be endless trouble and delay. The inspector of buildings would make trouble; complaints would be made of obstructing the streets and sidewalks, and injunctions would be issued.

So it was either to pay, or not construct.

Marx provided work for the needy, loaned money to the poor, sick and disabled, gave excursions and picnics in the summer: for all of this others paid, but it enabled him to hold the political control of the ward in the hollow of his hand.

The boss above him demanded that the councilmen from his ward should be men who would do his bidding without question.

The city boss, in turn, trafficked with the larger public contracts, and with the granting and extensions of franchises. It was a fruitful field, for there was none above him with whom he was compelled to divide.

The State boss treated the city bosses with much consideration, for he was more or less dependent upon them, his power consisting largely of the sum of their power.

The State boss dealt in larger things, and became a national figure. He was more circumspect in his methods, for he had a wider constituency and a more intelligent opposition.

The local bosses were required to send to the legislature "loyal" party men who did not question the leadership of the State boss.

The big interests preferred having only one man to deal with, which simplified matters; consequently they were strong aids in helping him retain his power.

Any measure they desired passed by the legislature was first submitted to him, and he would prune it until he felt he could

put it through without doing too great violence to public sentiment.

The citizens at large do not scrutinize measures closely; they
are too busy in their own vineyards to bother greatly about
things which only remotely or indirectly concern them.

This selfish attitude and indifference of our people has made
the boss and his methods possible. The "big interests" recipro-
cate in many and devious ways, ways subtle enough to seem
not dishonest even if exposed to public view.

So that by early education I was taught to think that the despoliation of the public, in certain ways, was a legitimate industry.

Later, I knew better, but I had already started my plow in the
furrow, and it was hard to turn back. I wanted money and I
wanted power, and I could see both in the career before me.

It was not long, of course, before I had discernment enough
to see that I was not being employed for my legal ability. My
income was practically made from retainers, and I was seldom
called upon to do more than to use my influence so that my
client should remain undisturbed in the pursuit of his business,
be it legitimate or otherwise.

Young as I was, Marx soon offered me a seat in the Council.
It was my first proffer of office, but I declined it. I did not want
to be identified with a body for which I had such a supreme
contempt.

My aim was higher. Marx, though, was sincere in his desire
to further my fortunes, for he had no son, and his affection for
my father and me was genuine.

I frankly told him the direction in which my ambition lay,
and he promised me his cordial assistance. I wanted to get beyond ward politics, and in touch with the city boss.

It was my idea that, if I could maintain myself with him, I

would in time ask him to place me within the influence of the State boss, where my field of endeavor would be as wide as my abilities would justify.

I did not lose my identity with my ward, but now my work covered all Philadelphia, and my retainers became larger and more numerous, for I was within the local sphere of the "big interests."

At that time the boss was a man by the name of Hardy. He was born in the western part of the State, but came to Philadelphia when a boy, his mother having married the second time a man named Metz, who was then City Treasurer and who afterwards became Mayor.

Hardy was a singular man for a boss; small of frame, with features almost effeminate, and with anything but a robust constitution, he did a prodigious amount of work.

He was not only taciturn to an unusual degree, but he seldom wrote, or replied to letters. Yet he held an iron grip upon the organization.

His personal appearance and quiet manners inspired many ambitious underlings to try to dislodge him, but their failure was signal and complete.

He had what was, perhaps, the most perfectly organized machine against which any municipality had ever had the misfortune to contend.

Hardy made few promises and none of them rash, but no man could truthfully say that he ever broke one. I feel certain that he would have made good his spoken word even at the expense of his fortune or political power.

Then, too, he played fair, and his henchmen knew it. He had no favorites whom he unduly rewarded at the expense of the more efficient. He had likes and dislikes as other men, but his judgment was never warped by that. Success meant advancement, failure meant retirement.

And he made his followers play fair. There were certain rules of the game that had to be observed, and any infraction thereof meant punishment.

The big, burly fellows he had under him felt pride in his physical insignificance, and in the big brain that had never known defeat.

When I became close to him, I asked him why he had never expanded; that he must have felt sure that he could have spread his jurisdiction throughout the State, and that the labor in the broader position must be less than in the one he occupied.

His reply was characteristic of the man. He said he was not where he was from choice, that environment and opportunity had forced him into the position he occupied, but that once there, he owed it to his followers to hold it against all comers. He said that he would have given it up long ago, if it had not been for this feeling of obligation to those who loved and trusted him. To desert them, and to make new responsibilities, was unthinkable from his viewpoint.

That which I most wondered at in Hardy was, his failure to comprehend that the work he was engaged in was dishonest. I led cautiously up to this one day, and this was his explanation:

"The average American citizen refuses to pay attention to civic affairs, contenting himself with a general growl at the tax rate, and the character and inefficiency of public officials. He seldom takes the trouble necessary to form the Government to suit his views.

"The truth is, he has no cohesive or well-digested views, it being too much trouble to form them. Therefore, some such organization as ours is essential. Being essential, then it must have funds with which to proceed, and the men devoting their lives to it must be recompensed, so the system we use is the best that can be devised under the circumstances.

"It is like the tariff and internal revenue taxes by which the National Government is run, that is, indirect. The citizen pays, but he does not know when he pays, nor how much he is paying.

"A better system could, perhaps, be devised in both instances, but this cannot be done until the people take a keener interest in their public affairs.

"Hardy was not a rich man, though he had every opportunity of being so. He was not avaricious, and his tastes and habits were simple, and he had no family to demand the extravagances that are undermining our national life. He was a vegetarian, and he thought, and perhaps rightly, that in a few centuries from now the killing of animals and the eating of their corpses would be regarded in the same way as we now think of cannibalism.

"He divided the money that came to him amongst his followers, and this was one of the mainsprings of his power.

"All things considered, it is not certain but that he gave Philadelphia as good government as her indifferent citizens deserved."

CHAPTER XXXV

Selwyn's Story, Continued

BY THE time I was thirty-six, I had accumulated what seemed to me then, a considerable fortune, and I had furthermore become Hardy's right-hand man.

He had his forces divided in several classes, of choice I was ranged among those whose duties were general and not local. I therefore had a survey of the city as a whole, and was not infrequently in touch with the masters of the State at large.

Hardy concerned himself about my financial welfare to the extent of now and then inquiring whether my income was satisfactory, and the nature of it. I assured him that it was and that he need have no further thought of me in that connection.

I told him that I was more ambitious to advance politically than financially, and, while expressing my gratitude for all he had done for me and my keen regret at the thought of leaving him, I spoke again of my desire to enter State politics.

Some six years before I had married the daughter of a State Senator, a man who was then seeking the gubernatorial nomination.

On my account, Hardy gave him cordial support, but the State boss had other plans, and my father-in-law was shelved "for the moment," as the boss expressed it, for one who suited his purposes better.

Both Hardy, my father-in-law, and their friends resented this action, because the man selected was not in line for the place and the boss was not conforming to the rules of the game.

They wanted to break openly and immediately, but I advised delay until we were strong enough to overthrow him.

The task of quietly organizing an effective opposition to the State boss was left to me, and although I lost no time, it was a year before I was ready to make the fight.

In the meanwhile, the boss had no intimation of the revolt. My father-in-law and Hardy had, by my direction, complied with all the requests that he made upon them, and he thought himself never more secure.

I went to the legislature that year in accordance with our plans, and announced myself a candidate for speaker. I did this without consulting the boss and purposely. He had already selected another man, and had publicly committed himself to his candidacy, which was generally considered equivalent to an election.

The candidate was a weak man, and if the boss had known the extent of the opposition that had developed, he would have made a stronger selection. As it was, he threw not only the weight of his own influence for his man and again irrevocably committed himself, but he had his creature, the Governor, do likewise.

My strength was still not apparent, for I had my forces well in hand, and while I had a few declare themselves for me, the major part were non-committal, and spoke in cautious terms of general approval of the boss's candidate.

The result was a sensation. I was elected by a safe, though small, majority, and, as a natural result, the boss was deposed and I was proclaimed his successor.

I had found in organizing the revolt that there were many who had grievances which, from fear, they had kept hidden but when they were shown that they could safely be revenged, they eagerly took advantage of the opportunity.

So, in one campaign, I burst upon the public as the party leader, and the question was now, how would I use it and could I hold it.

Chapter XXXVI

Selwyn's Story, Continued

FLUSHED though I was with victory, and with the flattery of friends, time servers and sycophants in my ears, I felt a deep sympathy for the boss. He was as a sinking ship and as such deserted. Yesterday a thing for envy, to-day an object of pity.

I wondered how long it would be before I, too, would be stranded.

The interests, were, of course, among the first to congratulate me and to assure me of their support.

During that session of the legislature, I did not change the character of the legislation, or do anything very different from the usual. I wanted to feel my seat more firmly under me before attempting the many things I had in mind.

I took over into my camp all those that I could reasonably trust, and strengthened my forces everywhere as expeditiously as possible. I weeded out the incompetents, of whom there were many, and replaced them by big-hearted, loyal and energetic men, who had easy consciences when it came to dealing with the public affairs of either municipalities, counties or the State.

Of necessity, I had to use some who were vicious and dishonest, and who would betray me in a moment if their interests led that way. But of these there were few in my personal organization, though from experience, I knew their kind permeated the municipal machines to a large degree.

The lessons learned from Hardy were of value to me now. I was liberal to my following at the expense of myself, and I played the game fair as they knew it.

I declined re-election to the next legislature, because the office was not commensurate with the dignity of the position I held as party leader, and again, because the holding of state office was now a perilous undertaking.

In taking over the machine from the late boss, and in molding it into an almost personal following I found it not only loosely put together, but inefficient for my more ambitious purposes.

After giving it four or five years of close attention, I was satisfied with it, and I had no fear of dislodgment.

I had found that the interests were not paying anything like a commensurate amount for the special privileges they were getting, and I more than doubled the revenue obtained by the deposed boss.

This, of course, delighted my henchmen, and bound them more closely to me.

I also demanded and received information in advance of any extensions of railroads, standard or interurban, of contemplated improvements of whatsoever character, and I doled out this information to those of my followers in whose jurisdiction lay such territory.

My own fortune I augmented by advance information regarding the appreciation of stocks. If an amalgamation of two important institutions was to occur, or if they were to be put upon a dividend basis, or if the dividend rate was to be increased, I was told, not only in advance of the public, but in advance of the stockholders themselves.

All such information I held in confidence even from own followers, for it was given me with such understanding.

My next move was to get into national politics. I became something of a factor at the national convention, by swinging Pennsylvania's vote at a critical time; the result being the nomination of the now President, consequently my relations with him were most cordial.

The term of the senior Senator from our State was about to expire, and, although he was well advanced in years, he desired re-election.

I decided to take his seat for myself, so I asked the President to offer him an ambassadorship. He did not wish to make the change, but when he understood that it was that or nothing, he gracefully acquiesced in order that he might be saved the humiliation of defeat.

When he resigned, the Governor offered me the appointment for the unexpired term. It had only three months to run before the legislature met to elect his successor.

I told him that I could not accept until I had conferred with my friends. I had no intention of refusing, but I wanted to seem to defer to the judgment of my lieutenants.

I called them to the capital singly, and explained that I could be of vastly more service to the organization were I at Washington, and I arranged with them to convert the rank and file to this view.

Each felt that the weight of my decision rested upon himself, and their vanity was greatly pleased. I was begged not to renounce the leadership, and after persuasion, this I promised not to do.

As a matter of fact, it was never my intention to release my hold upon the State, thus placing myself in another's power.

So I accepted the tender of the Senatorship, and soon after, when the legislature met, I was elected for the full term.

I was in as close touch with my State at Washington as I was before, for I spent a large part of my time there.

I was not in Washington long before I found that the Government was run by a few men; that outside of this little circle no one was of much importance.

It was my intention to break into it if possible, and my ambition now leaped so far as to want, not only to be of it, but later, to be IT.

I began my crusade by getting upon confidential terms with the President.

One night, when we were alone in his private study, I told him of the manner and completeness of my organization in Pennsylvania. I could see he was deeply impressed. He had been elected by an uncomfortably small vote, and he was, I knew, looking for someone to manage the next campaign, provided he again received the nomination.

The man who had done this work in the last election was broken in health, and had gone to Europe for an indefinite stay.

The President questioned me closely, and ended by asking me to undertake the direction of his campaign for re-nomination, and later to manage the campaign for his election in the event he was again the party's candidate.

I was flattered by the proffer, and told him so, but I was guarded in its acceptance. I wanted him to see more of me, hear more of my methods and to become, as it were, the suppliant.

This condition was soon brought about, and I entered into my new relations with him under the most favorable circumstances.

If I had readily acquiesced he would have assumed the air of favoring me, as it was, the rule was reversed.

He was overwhelmingly nominated and re-elected, and for the result he generously gave me full credit.

I was now well within the charmed circle, and within easy reach of my further desire to have no rivals. This came about naturally and without friction.

The interests, of course, were soon groveling at my feet, and, heavy as my demands were, I sometimes wondered like Clive at my own moderation.

The rest of my story is known to you. I had tightened a nearly invisible coil around the people, which held them fast, while the interests despoiled them. We overdid it, and you came with the conscience of the great majority of the American people back of you, and swung the Nation again into the moorings intended by the Fathers of the Republic.

When Selwyn had finished, the fire had burned low, and it was only now and then that his face was lighted by the flickering flames revealing a sadness that few had ever seen there before.

Perhaps he saw in the dying embers something typical of his life as it now was. Perhaps he longed to recall his youth and with it the strength, the nervous force and the tireless thought that he had used to make himself what he was.

When life is so nearly spilled as his, things are measured differently, and what looms large in the beginning becomes but the merest shadow when the race has been run.

As he contemplated the silent figure, Philip Dru felt something of regret himself, for he now knew the groundwork of the man, and he was sure that under other conditions, a career could have been wrought more splendid than that of any of his fellows.

CHAPTER XXXVII

The Cotton Corner

IN MODELING the laws, Dru called to the attention of those boards that were doing that work, the so-called "loan sharks," and told them to deal with them with a heavy hand. By no sort of subterfuge were they to be permitted to be usurious. By their nefarious methods of charging the maximum legal rate of interest and then exacting a commission for monthly renewals of loans, the poor and the dependent were oftentimes made to pay several hundred per cent interest per annum. The criminal code was to be invoked and protracted terms in prison, in addition to fines, were to be used against them.

He also called attention to a lesser, though serious, evil, of the practice of farmers, mine-owners, lumbermen and other employers of ignorant labor, of making advances of food, clothing and similar necessities to their tenants or workmen, and charging them extortionate prices therefor, thus securing the use of their labor at a cost entirely incommensurate with its value.

Stock, cotton and produce exchanges as then conducted came under the ban of the Administrator's displeasure, and he indicated his intention of reforming them to the extent of prohibiting, under penalty of fine and imprisonment, the selling either short or long, stocks, bonds, commodities of whatsoever character, or anything of value.

Banks, corporations or individuals lending money to any corporation or individual whose purpose it was known to be to violate this law, should be deemed as guilty as the actual offender and should be as heavily punished.

An immediate enforcement of this law was made because,

just before the Revolution, there was carried to a successful conclusion a gigantic but iniquitous cotton corner. Some twenty or more adventurous millionaires, led by one of the boldest speculators of those times, named Hawkins, planned and succeeded in cornering cotton.

It seemed that the world needed a crop of 16,000,000 bales, and while the yield for the year was uncertain it appeared that the crop would run to that figure and perhaps over. Therefore, prices were low and spot-cotton was selling around eight cents, and futures for the distant months were not much higher.

By using all the markets and exchanges and by exercising much skill and secrecy, Hawkins succeeded in buying two million bales of actual cotton, and ten million bales of futures at an approximate average of nine and a half cents. He had the actual cotton stored in relatively small quantities throughout the South, much of it being on the farms and at the gins where it was bought. Then, in order to hide his identity, he had incorporated a company called "The Farmers' Protective Association."

Through one of his agents he succeeded in officering it with well-known Southerners, who knew only that part of the plan which contemplated an increase in prices, and were in sympathy with it.

He transferred his spot-cotton to this company, the stock of which he himself held through his dummies, *and then had his agents burn the entire two million bales*. The burning was done quickly and with spectacular effect, and the entire commercial world, both in America and abroad, were astounded by the act.

Once before in isolated instances the cotton planter had done this, and once the farmers of the West, discouraged by low prices, had used corn for fuel. That, however, was done on a small scale. But to deliberately burn one hundred million dollars worth of property was almost beyond the scope of the imagination.

The result was a cotton panic, and Hawkins succeeded in closing out his futures at an average price of fifteen cents, thereby netting twenty-five dollars a bale, and making for himself and fellow buccaneers one hundred and fifty million dollars.

After amazement came indignation at such frightful abuse of concentrated wealth. Those of Wall Street that were not caught, were open in their expressions of admiration for Hawkins, for of such material are their heroes made.

CHAPTER XXXVIII

Universal Suffrage

AT THE end of the first quarter of the present century, twenty of the forty-eight States had Woman Suffrage, and Administrator Dru decided to give it to the Nation. In those twenty States, as far as he had observed, there had been no change for the better in the general laws, nor did the officials seem to have higher standards of efficiency than in those States that still denied to women the right to vote, but he noticed that there were more special laws bearing on the moral and social side of life, and that police regulation was better. Upon the whole, Dru thought the result warranted universal franchise without distinction of race, color or sex.

He believed that, up to the present time, a general franchise had been a mistake and that there should have been restrictions and qualifications, but education had become so general, and the condition of the people had advanced to such an extent, that it was now warranted.

It had long seemed to Dru absurd that the ignorant, and, as a rule, more immoral male, should have such an advantage over the educated, refined and intelligent female. Where laws discriminated at all, it was almost always against rather than in favor of women; and this was true to a much greater extent in Europe and elsewhere than in the United States. Dru had a profound sympathy for the effort women were making to get upon an equality with men in the race for life: and he believed that with the franchise would come equal opportunity and equal pay for the same work.

America, he hoped, might again lead in the uplift of the sex, and the example would be a distinct gain to women in those

177

less forward countries where they were still largely considered as inferior to and somewhat as chattels to man.

Then, too, Dru had an infinite pity for the dependent and submerged life of the generality of women. Man could ask woman to mate, but women were denied this privilege, and, even when mated, oftentimes a life of never ending drudgery followed.

Dru believed that if women could ever become economically independent of man, it would, to a large degree, mitigate the social evil.

They would then no longer be compelled to marry, or be a charge upon unwilling relatives or, as in desperation they sometimes did, lead abandoned lives.

CHAPTER XXXIX

A Negative Government

UPON assuming charge of the affairs of the Republic, the Administrator had largely retained the judiciary as it was then constituted, and he also made but few changes in the personnel of State and Federal officials, therefore there had, as yet, been no confusion in the public's business. Everything seemed about as usual, further than there were no legislative bodies sitting, and the function of law making was confined to one individual, the Administrator himself.

Before putting the proposed laws into force, he wished them thoroughly worked out and digested. In the meantime, however, he was constantly placing before his Cabinet and Commissioners suggestions looking to the betterment of conditions, and he directed that these suggestions should be molded into law. In order that the people might know what further measures he had in mind for their welfare, other than those already announced, he issued the following address:

"It is my purpose," said he, "not to give to you any radical or ill-digested laws. I wish rather to cull that which is best from the other nations of the earth, and let you have the benefit of their thought and experience. One of the most enlightened foreign students of our Government has rightly said that '*America is the most undemocratic of democratic countries.*' We have been living under a Government of negation, a Government with an executive with more power than any monarch, a Government having a Supreme Court, clothed with greater authority than any similar body on earth; therefore, we have lagged behind other nations in democracy. Our Government is, perhaps, less responsive to the will of the people than that of almost any of the civilized nations. Our Constitution and our laws served us well for the first hundred years of our existence, but under the conditions of to-day they are not only obsolete, but even grotesque. It is nearly impossible for the desires of our people to find expression into law. In the latter part of the last century many will remember that an income tax was wanted. After many vicissitudes, a measure embodying that idea was passed by both Houses of Congress and was signed by the Executive. But that did not give to us an income tax. The Supreme Court found the law unconstitutional, and we have been vainly struggling since to obtain relief.

"If a well-defined majority of the people of England, of France, of Italy, or of Germany had wanted such a law they could have gotten it with reasonable celerity. Our House of Representatives is supposed to be our popular law-making body, and yet its members do not convene until a year and one month from the time they are elected. No matter how pressing the issue upon which a majority of them are chosen, more than a year must elapse before they may begin their endeavors to carry out the will of the people. When a bill covering the question at issue is finally introduced in the House, it is referred to a committee, and that body may hold it at its pleasure.

"If, in the end, the House should pass the bill, that probably becomes the end of it, for the Senate may kill it.

"If the measure passes the Senate it is only after it has again been referred to a committee and then back to a conference committee of both Senate and House, and returned to each for final passage.

"When all this is accomplished at a single session, it is unusually expeditious, for measures, no matter how important, are often carried over for another year.

"If it should at last pass both House and Senate there is the

Executive veto to be considered. If, however, the President signs the bill and it becomes a law, it is perhaps but short-lived, for the Supreme Court is ever present with its Damoclean sword.

"These barriers and interminable delays have caused the demand for the initiative, referendum and recall. That clumsy weapon was devised in some States largely because the people were becoming restless and wanted a more responsive Government.

"I am sure that I shall be able to meet your wishes in a much simpler way, and yet throw sufficient safeguards around the new system to keep it from proving hurtful, should an attack of political hysteria overtake you.

"However, there has never been a time in our history when a majority of our people have not thought right on the public questions that came before them, and there is no reason to believe that they will think wrong now.

"The interests want a Government hedged with restrictions, such as we have been living under, and it is easy to know why, with the example of the last administration fresh in the minds of all.

"A very distinguished lawyer, once Ambassador to Great Britain, is reported as saying on Lincoln's birthday: 'The Constitution is an instrument designedly drawn by the founders of this Government providing safeguards to prevent any inroads by popular excitement or frenzy of the moment.' And later in the speech he says: 'But I have faith in the sober judgment of the American people, that they will reject these radical changes, etc.'

"If he had faith in the sober judgment of the American people, why not trust them to a measurable extent with the conduct of their own affairs?

"The English people, for a century or more, have had such direction as I now propose that you shall have, and for more than half a century the French people have had like power. They have in no way abused it, and yet the English and French Electorate surely are not more intelligent, or have better self control, or more sober judgment than the American citizenship.

"Another thing to which I desire your attention called is the dangerous power possessed by the President in the past, but of which the new Constitution will rob him.

"The framers of the Constitution lived in an atmosphere of autocracy and they could not know, as we do now, the danger of placing in one man's hands such enormous power, and have him so far from the reach of the people, that before they could dispossess him he might, if conditions were favorable, establish a dynasty.

"It is astounding that we have allowed a century and a half go by without limiting both his term and his power.

"In addition to giving you a new Constitution and laws that will meet existing needs, there are many other things to be done, some of which I shall briefly outline. I have arranged to have a survey made of the swamp lands throughout the United States. From reliable data which I have gathered, I am confident that an area as large as the State of Ohio can be reclaimed, and at a cost that will enable the Government to sell it to homeseekers for less than one-fourth what they would have to pay elsewhere for similar land.

"Under my personal direction, I am having prepared an old-age pension law and also a laborers' insurance law, covering loss in cases of illness, incapacity and death.

"I have a commission working on an efficient cooperative system of marketing the products of small farms and factories. The small producers throughout America are not getting a sufficient return for their products, largely because they lack the facilities for marketing them properly. By coöperation they will be placed upon an equal footing with the large producers and small investments that heretofore have given but a meager return will become profitable.

"I am also planning to inaugurate coöperative loan societies in every part of the Union, and I have appointed a commissioner to instruct the people as to their formation and conduct and to explain their beneficent results.

"In many parts of Europe such societies have reached very high proficiency, and have been the means of bringing prosperity to communities that before their establishment had gone into decay.

"Many hundred millions of dollars have been loaned through these societies and, while only a fractional part of their members would be considered good for even the smallest amount at a bank, the losses to the societies on loans to their members have been almost negligible; less indeed than regular bankers could show on loans to their clients. And yet it enables those that are almost totally without capital to make a fair living for themselves and families.

"It is my purpose to establish bureaus through the congested portions of the United States where men and women in search of employment can register and be supplied with information as to where and what kind of work is obtainable. And if no work is to be had, I shall arrange that every indigent person that is honest and industrious *shall be given employment by the Federal, State, County or Municipal Government as the case may be*. Furthermore, it shall in the future be unlawful for any employer of labor to require more than eight hours work a day, and then only for six days a week. Conditions as are now found in the great manufacturing centers where employés are worked twelve hours a day, seven days in the week, and receive wages inadequate for even an eight hour day shall be no longer possible.

"If an attempt is made to reduce wages because of shorter hours or for any other cause, the employé shall have the right to go before a magistrate and demand that the amount of wage be adjusted there, either by the magistrate himself or by a jury if demanded by either party.

"Where there are a large number of employés affected, they can act through their unions or societies, if needs be, and each party at issue may select an arbitrator and the two so chosen may agree upon a third, or they may use the courts and juries, as may be preferred.

"This law shall be applicable to women as well as to men, and to every kind of labor. I desire to make it clear that the policy of this Government is that every man or woman who desires work shall have it, even if the Government has to give it, and I wish it also understood that an adequate wage must be paid for labor.

"Labor is no longer to be classed as an inert commodity to be bought and sold by the law of supply and demand, but the *human equation shall hereafter be the commanding force in all agreements between man and capital.*

"There is another matter to which I shall give my earnest attention and that is the reformation of the study and practice of medicine. It is well known that we are far behind England, Germany and France in the protection of our people from incompetent physicians and quackery. There is no more competent, no more intelligent or advanced men in the world than our American physicians and surgeons of the first class.

"But the incompetent men measurably drag down the high standing of the profession. A large part of our medical schools and colleges are entirely unfit for the purposes intended, and each year they grant diplomas to hundreds of ignorant young men and women and license them to prey upon a more or less helpless people.

"The number of physicians per inhabitant is already ridiculously large, many times more than is needful, or than other countries where the average of the professions ranks higher, deem necessary.

"I feel sure that the death list in the United States from the mistakes of these incompetents is simply appalling.

"I shall create a board of five eminent men, two of whom shall be physicians, one shall be a surgeon, one a scientist and the other shall be a great educator, and to this board I shall give the task of formulating a plan by which the spurious medical colleges and medical men can be eradicated from our midst.

"I shall call the board's attention to the fact that it is of as much importance to have men of fine natural ability as it is to give them good training, and, if it is practicable, I shall ask them to require some sort of adequate mental examination that will measurably determine this.

"I have a profound admiration for the courage, the nobility and philanthropy of the profession as a whole, and I do not want its honor tarnished by those who are mercenary and unworthy.

"In conclusion I want to announce that pensions will be given to those who fought on either side in the late war without distinction or reservation. However, it is henceforth to be the policy of this Government, so far as I may be able to shape it, that only those in actual need of financial aid shall receive pensions and to them it shall be given, whether they have or have not been disabled in consequence of their services to the nation. But to offer financial aid to the rich and well to do, is to offer an insult, for it questions their patriotism. Although the first civil war was ended over sixty years ago, yet that pension roll still draws heavily upon the revenue of the Nation. Its history has been a rank injustice to the noble armies of Grant and his lieutenants, the glory of whose achievements is now the common heritage of a United Country."

CHAPTER XL

A Departure in Battleships

DRU invited the Strawns to accompany him to Newport News to witness the launching of a new type of battleship. It was said to be, and probably was, impenetrable. Experts who had tested a model built on a large scale had declared that this invention would render obsolete every battleship in existence. The principle was this: Running back from the bow for a distance of 60 feet only about 4 feet of the hull showed above the water line, and this part of the deck was concaved and of the smoothest, hardest steel. Then came several turreted sections upon which guns were mounted. Around these turrets ran rims of polished steel, two feet in width and six inches thick. These rims began four feet from the water line and ran four feet above the level of the turret decks. The rims were so nicely adjusted with ball bearings that the smallest blow would send them spinning around, therefore a shell could not penetrate because it would glance off.

Although the trip to the Newport News Dock yards was made in a Navy hydroaeroplane it took several hours, and Gloria used the occasion to urge upon Dru the rectification of some abuses of which she had special knowledge.

"Philip," she said, "when I was proselytizing among the rich, it came to me to include the employer of women labor. I found but few who dissented from my statement of facts, but the answer was that trade conditions, the demand of customers for cheaper garments and articles, made relief impracticable. Perhaps their profits are on a narrow basis, Philip; but the volume of their business is the touchstone of their success, for how otherwise could so many become millionaires? Just what the remedy is I do not know, but I want to give you the facts so that in recasting the laws you may plan something to alleviate a grievous wrong."

"It is strange, Gloria, how often your mind and mine are caught by the same current, and how they drift in the same direction. It was only a few days ago that I picked up one of O. Henry's books. In his 'Unfinished Story' he tells of a man who dreamed that he died and was standing with a crowd of prosperous looking angels before Saint Peter, when a policeman came up and taking him by the wing asked: 'Are you with that bunch?'

"'Who are they?' asked the man.

"'Why,' said the policeman, 'they are the men who hired working girls and paid 'em five or six dollars a week to live on. Are you one of the bunch?'

"'Not on your immortality,' answered the man. 'I'm only the fellow who set fire to an orphan asylum, and murdered a blind man for his pennies.'

"Some years ago when I first read that story, I thought it was humor, now I know it to be pathos. Nothing, Gloria, will give me greater pleasure than to try to think out a solution to this problem, and undertake its application."

Gloria then gave more fully the conditions governing female labor. The unsanitary surroundings, the long hours and the inadequate wage, the statistics of refuge societies showed, drove an appalling number of women and girls to the streets. — No matter how hard they worked they could not earn sufficient to clothe and feed themselves properly. After a deadly day's work, many of them found stimulants of various kinds the cheapest means of bringing comfort to their weary bodies and hope-lost souls, and then the next step was the beginning of the end.

By now they had come to Newport News and the launching of the battleship was made as Gloria christened her *Columbia*. After the ceremonies were over it became necessary at once to return to Washington, for at noon of the next day there was to be dedicated the Colossal Arch of Peace. Ten years before, the Government had undertaken this work and had slowly executed it, carrying out the joint conception of the foremost architect in America and the greatest sculptor in the world. Strangely enough, the architect was a son of New England, and the Sculptor was from and of the South.

Upon one face of the arch were three heroic figures. Lee on the one side, Grant on the other, with Fame in the center, holding out a laurel wreath with either hand to both Grant and Lee. Among the figures clustered around and below that of Grant, were those of Sherman, Sheridan, Thomas and Hancock, and among those around and below that of Lee, were Stonewall Jackson, the two Johnstons, Forrest, Pickett and Beauregard. Upon the other face of the arch there was in the center a heroic figure of Lincoln and gathered around him on either side were those Statesmen of the North and South who took part in that titanic civil conflict that came so near to dividing our Republic.

Below Lincoln's figure was written: "With malice toward none, with charity for all." Below Grant, was his dying injunction to his fellow countrymen: "Let us have peace." But the silent and courtly Lee left no message that would fit his gigantic mold.

CHAPTER XLI

The New National Constitution

BESIDES the laws and reforms already enumerated, the following is in brief the plan for the General Government that Philip Dru outlined and carried through as Administrator of the Republic, and which, in effect, was made a part of the new constitution.

I.

1. Every adult citizen of the United States, male or female, shall have the right to vote, and no state, county or municipality shall pass a law or laws infringing upon this right.

2. Any alien, male or female, who can read, write and speak English, and who has resided in the United States for ten years, may take out naturalization papers and become a citizen.[1]

3. No one shall be eligible for election as Executive, President, Senator, Representative or Judge of any court under the age of twenty-five years, and who is not a citizen of the United States.[2]

4. No one shall be eligible for any other office, National or State, who is at the time, or who has been within a period

---

[1]See Appendix
[2]See Appendix.

[3]See Appendix.

of five years preceding, a member of any Senate or Court.[3]

II

1. The several states shall be divided into districts of three hundred thousand inhabitants each, and each district so divided shall have one representative, and in order to give the widest latitude as to choice, there shall be no restrictions as to residence.[1]

2. The members of the House of Representatives shall be elected on the first Tuesday after the first Monday in November, and shall serve for a term of six years, subject to a recall at the end of each two years by a signed petition embracing one-third of the electorate of the district from which they were chosen.[2]

3. The House shall convene on the first Tuesday after the first Monday in January and shall never have more than five hundred members.[3]

4. The House of Representatives shall elect a Speaker whose term of office may be continuous at the pleasure of the majority. He shall preside over the House, but otherwise his functions shall be purely formal.

5. The House shall also choose an Executive, whose duties it shall be, under the direction of the House, to administer the Government. He may or may not be at the time of his election a member of the House, but he becomes an ex-officio

---

[1]See Appendix.
[2]See Appendix.
[3]See Appendix.

member by virtue thereof.

6. (a) The Executive shall have authority to select his Cabinet Officers from members of the House or elsewhere, other than from the Courts or Senates, and such Cabinet Officers shall by reason thereof, be ex-officio members of the House.

(b) Such officials are to hold their positions at the pleasure of the Executive and the Executive is to hold his at the pleasure of the majority of the House.

(c) In an address to the House, the Executive shall, within a reasonable time after his selection, outline his policy of Government, both domestic and foreign.

(d) He and his Cabinet may frame bills covering the suggestions made in his address, or any subsequent address that he may think proper to make, and introduce and defend them in the House. Measures introduced by the Executive or members of his Cabinet are not to be referred to committees, but are to be considered by the House as a whole, and their consideration shall have preference over measures introduced by other members.

7. All legislation shall originate in the House.

III

1. The Senate shall consist of one member from each State, and shall be elected for life, by direct vote of the people, and shall be subject to recall by a majority vote of the electors of his State at the end of any five-year period of his term.[1]

---

[1]See Appendix.

2. (a) Every measure passed by the House, other than those relating *solely* to the raising of revenue for the current needs of the Government and the expenditure thereof, shall go to the Senate for approval.

(b) The Senate may approve a measure by a majority vote and then it becomes a law, or they may make suggestions regarding the amendment as may seem to them pertinent, and return it to the House to accept or reject as they may see fit.

(c) The Senate may reject a measure by a majority vote. If the Senate reject a measure, the House shall have the right to dissolve and go before the people for their decision.

(d) If the country approves the measure by returning a House favorable to it, then, upon its passage by the House *in the same form as when rejected by the Senate*, it shall become law.

3. (a) A Senator may be impeached by a majority vote of the Supreme Court, upon an action approved by the House and brought by the Executive or any member of his Cabinet.
    (b) A Senator must retire at the age of seventy years, and he shall be suitably pensioned.

IV

1. The President shall be chosen by a majority vote of all the electors. His term shall be for ten years and he shall be ineligible for re-election, but after retirement he shall receive a pension.

2. His duties shall be almost entirely formal and ceremonial.

3. In the event of a hiatus in the Government from any source whatsoever, it shall be his duty immediately to call an election, and in the meantime act as Executive until the regularly elected authorities can again assume charge of the Government.

CHAPTER XLII

New State Constitutions

To THE States, Administrator Dru gave governments in all essentials like that of the nation.

In brief the State instruments held the following provisions:

1. The House of Representatives shall consist of one member for every fifty thousand inhabitants, and never shall exceed a membership of two hundred in any State.

2. Representatives shall be elected for a term of two years, but not more than one session shall be held during their tenure of office unless called in special session by the Speaker of the House with approval of the Governor.

3. Representatives shall be elected in November, and the House shall convene on the first Tuesday after the first Monday in January to sit during its own pleasure.

4. Representatives shall make rules for their self-government and shall be the general state law making body.

II

1. The Senate shall be composed of one member from each congressional district, but there shall never be less than five nor more than fifty in any State Senate.

2. Senators shall be elected for a term of ten years subject to

recall at the end of each two years, by petition signed by a majority of the electorate of their district.

3. (a) No legislation shall originate in the Senate. Its function is to advise as to measures sent there by the House, to make suggestions and such amendments as might seem pertinent, and return to the House, for its final action.

(b) When a bill is sent to the Senate by the House, if approved, it shall become law, if disapproved, it shall be returned to the House with the objections stated.

(c) If the House considers a measure of sufficient importance, it may dissolve immediately and let the people pass upon it, or they may wait until a regular election for popular action.

(d) If the people approve the measure, the House *must enact it in the same form as when disapproved by the Senate*, and it shall then become a law.

III

1. (a) The Governor shall be elected by a direct vote of all the people.

(b) His term of office shall be six years, and he shall be ineligible for re-election. He shall be subject to recall at the end of every two years by a majority vote of the State.[1]

2. (a) He shall have no veto power or other control over legislation, and shall not make any suggestions or recommendations in regard thereto.

---

[1]See Appendix.

198

(b) His function shall be purely executive. He may select his own council or fellow commissioners for the different governmental departments, and they shall hold their positions at his pleasure.

(c) All the Governor's appointees shall be confirmed by the Senate before they may assume office.

(d) The Governor may be held strictly accountable by the people for the honest, efficient and economical conduct of the government, due allowance being made for the fact that he is in no way responsible for the laws under which he must work.

(e) It shall be his duty also to report to the legislature at each session, giving an account of his stewardship regarding the enforcement of the laws, the conduct of the different departments, etc., etc., and making an estimate for the financial budget required for the two years following.

3.   (a) There shall be a Pardon Board of three members who shall pass upon all matters relating to the Penal Service.

(b) This Board shall be nominated by the Governor and confirmed by the Senate. After their confirmation, the Governor shall have no further jurisdiction over them.

(c) They shall hold office for six years and shall be ineligible for reappointment.

(d) They shall be subject to removal by the joint action of the House of Representatives and the Senate for neglect or failure of duty.

Besides the skeleton outline given of the simplified National and State Governments, the Administrator included a number of other provisions which seemed necessary to meet existing conditions. One of which was in regard to the civil service in the National, State, County and Municipal governments. Primarily, every employe of the people was to be subject to the requirements of the service, but there were to be no removals except for good and sufficient cause. Moreover, it was stipulated that reasons for dismissal must be made public if requested by the official or employé dismissed.

Dru recommended to the states and municipalities that they pay their officials sufficiently well to induce men of good ability to accept office. He pointed out that they could afford to be liberal in compensation given, because the number of officials would be greatly reduced, and because the general scheme of government would be vastly more efficient and economical than any which had heretofore been in force.

CHAPTER XLIII

The Rule of the Bosses

GENERAL DRU was ever fond of talking to Senator Selwyn. He found his virile mind a never-failing source of information. Busy as they both were they often met and exchanged opinions.

In answer to a question from Dru, Selwyn said that while Pennsylvania and a few other States had been more completely under the domination of bosses than others, still the system permeated everywhere.

In some States a railroad held the power, but exercised it through an individual or individuals.

In another State, a single corporation held it, and yet again, it was often held by a corporate group acting together. In many States one individual dominated public affairs and more often for good than evil.

The people simply would not take enough interest in their Government to exercise the right of control.

Those who took an active interest were used as a part of the boss' tools, be he a benevolent one or otherwise.

"The delegates go to the conventions," said Selwyn, "and think they have something to do with the naming of the nominees, and the making of the platforms. But the astute boss has planned all that far in advance, the candidates are selected and the platform written and both are 'forced' upon the unsuspecting delegate, much as the card shark forced his cards upon his victim. It is all seemingly in the open and above the boards, but as a matter of fact quite the reverse is true.

"At conventions it is usual to select some man who has always been honored and respected, and elect him chairman of the platform committee. He is pleased with the honor and is ready to do the bidding of the man to whom he owes it.

"The platform has been read to him and he has been committed to it before his appointment as chairman. Then a careful selection is made of delegates from the different senatorial districts and a good working majority of trusted followers is obtained for places on the committee. Someone nominates for chairman the 'honored and respected' and he is promptly elected.

"Another member suggests that the committee, as it stands, is too unwieldy to draft a platform, and makes a motion that the chairman be empowered to appoint a sub-committee of five to outline one and submit it to the committee as a whole.

"The motion is carried and the chairman appoints five of the 'tried and true.' There is then an adjournment until the sub-committee is ready to report.

"The five betake themselves to a room in some hotel and smoke, drink and swap stories until enough time has elapsed for a proper platform to be written.

"Then they report to the committee as a whole and, after some wrangling by the uninitiated, the platform is passed as the boss has written it without the addition of a single word.

"Sometimes it is necessary to place upon the sub-committee a recalcitrant or two. Then the method is somewhat different. The boss' platform is cut into separate planks and first one and then another of the faithful offers a plank, and after some discussion a majority of the committee adopt it. So when the sub-committee reports back there stands the boss' handiwork just as he has constructed it.

"Oftentimes there is no subterfuge, but the convention, as a whole, recognizes the pre-eminent ability of one man amongst them, and by common consent he is assigned the task."

Selwyn also told Dru that it was often the practice among corporations not to bother themselves about state politics further than to control the Senate.

This smaller body was seldom more than one-fourth as large as the House, and usually contained not more than twenty-five or thirty members.

Their method was to control a majority of the Senate and let the House pass such measures as it pleased, and the Governor recommend such laws as he thought proper. Then the Senate would promptly kill all legislation that in any way touched corporate interests.

Still another method which was used to advantage by the interests where they had not been vigilant in the protection of their "rights," and when they had no sure majority either in the House or Senate and no influence with the Governor, was to throw what strength they had to the stronger side in the factional fights that were always going on in every State and in every legislature.

Actual money, Selwyn said, was now seldom given in the relentless warfare which the selfish interests were ever waging against the people, but it was intrigue, the promise of place and power, and the ever effectual appeal to human vanity.

That part of the press which was under corporate control was often able to make or destroy a man's legislative and political career, and the weak and the vain and the men with shifty consciences, that the people in their fatuous indifference elect to make their laws, seldom fail to succumb to this subtle influence.

CHAPTER XLIV

One Cause of the High Cost of Living

IN ONE of their fireside talks, Selwyn told Dru that a potential weapon in the hands of those who had selfish purposes to subserve, was the long and confusing ballot.

"Whenever a change is suggested by which it can be shortened, and the candidates brought within easy review of the electorate, the objection is always raised," said Selwyn, "that the rights of the people are being invaded."

" 'Let the people rule,' is the cry," he said, "and the unthinking many believing that democratic government is being threatened, demand that they be permitted to vote for every petty officer.

"Of course quite the reverse is true," continued Selwyn, "for when the ballot is filled with names of candidates running for general and local offices, there is, besides the confusion, the usual trading. As a rule, interest centers on the local man, and there is less scrutiny of those candidates seeking the more important offices."

"While I had already made up my mind," said Dru, "as to the short ballot and a direct accountability to the people, I am glad to have you confirm the correctness of my views."

"You may take my word for it, General Dru, that the interests also desire large bodies of law makers instead of few. You may perhaps recall how vigorously they opposed the commission form of government for cities.

"Under the old system when there was a large council, no one was responsible. If a citizen had a grievance, and complained to his councilman, he was perhaps truthfully told that he was not to blame. He was sent from one member of the city government to the other, and unable to obtain relief, in sheer desperation, he gave up hope and abandoned his effort for justice. But under the commission form of government, none of the officials can shirk responsibility. Each is in charge of a department, and if there is inefficiency, it is easy to place the blame where it properly belongs.

"Under such a system the administration of public affairs becomes at once, simple, direct and business-like. If any outside corrupt influences seek to creep in, they are easy of detection and the punishment can be made swift and certain."

"I want to thank you again, Senator Selwyn, "for the help you have been to me in giving me the benefit of your ripe experience in public affairs," said Dru, "and there is another phase of the subject that I would like to discuss with you. I have thought long and seriously how to overcome the fixing of prices by individuals and corporations, and how the people may be protected from that form of robbery.

"When there is a monopoly or trust, it is easy to locate the offense, but it is a different proposition when one must needs deal with a large number of corporations and individuals, who, under the guise of competition, have an understanding, both as to prices and territory to be served.

"For instance, the coal dealers, at the beginning of winter, announce a fixed price for coal. If there are fifty of them and all are approached, not one of them will vary his quotation from the other forty-nine. If he should do so, the coal operators would be informed and the offending dealer would find, by some pretext or another, his supply cut off.

"We see the same condition regarding large supply and manufacturing concerns which cover the country with their very essential products. A keen rivalry is apparent, and competitive bids in sealed envelopes are made when requested, but as a matter of fact, we know that there is no competition. Can you give me any information upon this matter?"

"There are many and devious ways by which the law can be evaded and by which the despoliation of the public may be accomplished," said Selwyn. "The representatives of those large business concerns meet and a map of the United States is spread out before them. This map is regarded by them very much as if it were a huge pie that is to be divided according to the capacity of each to absorb and digest his share. The territory is not squared off, that is, taking in whole sections of contiguous country, but in a much more subtle way, so that the delusion of competition may be undisturbed. When several of these concerns are requested to make prices, they readily comply and seem eager for the order. The delusion extends even to their agents, who are as innocent as the would-be purchaser of the real conditions, and are doing their utmost to obtain the business. The concern in whose assigned territory the business originates, makes the price and informs its supposed rivals of its bid, so that they may each make one slightly higher."

"Which goes to show," said Dru, "how easy it is to exploit the public when there is harmony among the exploiters. There seems to me to be two evils involved in this problem, Senator Selwyn, one is the undue cost to the people, and the other, but lesser, evil, is the protection of incompetency.

"It is not the survival of the fittest, but an excess of profits, that enables the incompetent to live and thrive."

After a long and exhaustive study of this problem, the Administrator directed his legal advisers to incorporate his views into law.

No individual as such, was to be permitted to deal in what might be termed products of the natural resources of the country, unless he subjected himself to all the publicity and penalties that would accrue to a corporation, under the new corporate regulations.

Corporations, argued Dru, could be dealt with under the new laws in a way that, while fair to them, would protect the public. In the future, he reminded his commission, there would be upon the directorates a representative of either the National, State, or Municipal governments, and the books, and every transaction, would be open to the public. This would apply to both the owner of the raw material, be it mine, forest, or what not, as well as to the corporation or individual who distributed the marketable product.

It was Dru's idea that public opinion was to be invoked to aid in the task, and district attorneys and grand juries, throughout the country, were to be admonished to do their duty. If there was a fixity of prices in any commodity or product, or even approximately so, he declared, it would be prima facie evidence of a combination.

In this way, the Administrator thought the evil of pools and trust agreements could be eradicated, and a healthful competition, content with reasonable profits, established. If a single corporation, by its extreme efficiency, or from unusual conditions, should constitute a monopoly so that there was practically no competition, then it would be necessary, he thought, for the Government to fix a price reasonable to all interests involved.

Therefore it was not intended to put a limit on the size or the comprehensiveness of any corporation, further than that it should not stifle competition, except by greater efficiency in production and distribution. If this should happen, then the people and the Government would be protected by publicity, by their representative on the board of directors and by the fixing of prices, if necessary.

It had been shown by the career of one of the greatest industrial combinations that the world has yet known, that there was a limit where size and inefficiency met. The only way that this corporation could maintain its lead was through the devious paths of relentless monopoly.

Dru wanted America to contend for its share of the world's trade, and to enable it to accomplish this, he favored giving business the widest latitude consistent with the protection of the people.

When he assumed control of the Government, one of the many absurdities of the American economic system was the practical inhibition of a merchant marine. While the country was second to none in the value and quantity of production, yet its laws were so framed that it was dependent upon other nations for its transportation by sea; and its carrying trade was in no way commensurate with the dignity of the coast line and with the power and wealth of the Nation.

CHAPTER XLV

Burial Reform

AT ABOUT this time the wife of one of the Cabinet officers died, and Administrator Dru attended the funeral. There was an unusually large gathering, but it was plain that most of those who came did so from morbid curiosity. The poignant grief of the bereaved husband and children wrung the heartstrings of their many sympathetic friends. The lowering of the coffin, the fall of the dirt upon its cover, and the sobs of those around the grave, was typical of such occasions.

Dru was deeply impressed and shocked, and he thought to use his influence towards a reformation of such a cruel and unnecessary form of burial. When the opportunity presented itself, he directed attention to the objections to this method of disposing of the dead, and he suggested the formation in every community of societies whose purpose should be to use their influence towards making interments private, and towards the substitution of cremation for the unsanitary custom of burial in cemeteries. These societies were urged to point out the almost prohibitive expense the present method entailed upon the poor and those of moderate means. The buying of the lot and casket, the cost of the funeral itself, and the discarding of useful clothing in order to robe in black, were alike unnecessary. Some less dismal insignia of grief should be adopted, he said, that need not include the entire garb. Grief, he pointed out, and respect for the dead, were in no way better evidenced by such barbarous customs.

Rumor had it that scandal's cruel tongue was responsible for this good woman's death. She was one of the many victims that go to unhappy graves in order that the monstrous appetite for gossip may be appeased. If there be punishment after death, surely, the creator and disseminator of scandal will come to know the anger and contempt of a righteous God. The good and the bad are all of a kind to them. Their putrid minds see something vile in every action, and they leave the drippings of their evil tongues wherever they go. Some scandalmongers are merely stupid and vulgar, while others have a biting wit that cause them to be feared and hated. Rumors they repeat as facts, and to speculations they add what corroborative evidence is needed. The dropping of the eyelids, the smirk that is so full of insinuation is used to advantage where it is more effective than the downright lie. The burglar and the highwayman go frankly abroad to gather in the substance of others, and they stand ready to forfeit both life and liberty while in pursuit of nefarious gain. Yet it is a noble profession compared with that of the scandalmonger, and the murderer himself is hardly a more objectionable member of society than the character assassin.

CHAPTER XLVI

The Wise Disposition of a Fortune

IN ONE of their confidential talks, Selwyn told Dru that he had a fortune in excess of two hundred million dollars, and that while it was his intention to amply provide for his immediate family, and for those of his friends who were in need, he desired to use the balance of his money in the best way he could devise to help his fellowmen.

He could give for this purpose, he said, two hundred million dollars or more, for he did not want to provide for his children further than to insure their entire comfort, and to permit them to live on a scale not measurably different from what they had been accustomed.

He had never lived in the extravagant manner that was usual in men of his wealth, and his children had been taught to expect only a moderate fortune at his death. He was too wise a man not to know that one of the greatest burdens that wealth imposed, was the saving of one's children from its contaminations. He taught his sons that they were seriously handicapped by their expectations of even moderate wealth, and that unless they were alert and vigilant and of good habits, the boy who was working his own way upward would soon outstrip them. They were taught that they themselves, were the natural objects of pity and parental concern, and not their seemingly less fortunate brothers.

"Look among those whose parents have wealth and have given of it lavishly to their children," he said, "and count how few are valuable members of society or hold the respect of their fellows.

"On the other hand, look at the successful in every vocation

213

of life, and note how many have literally dug their way to success."

The more Dru saw of Selwyn, the better he liked him, and knowing the inner man, as he then did, the more did he marvel at his career. He and Selwyn talked long and earnestly over the proper disposition of his fortune. They both knew that it was hard to give wisely and without doing more harm than good. Even in providing for his friends, Selwyn was none too sure that he was conferring benefits upon them. Most of them were useful though struggling members of society, but should competency come to them, he wondered how many would continue as such. There was one, the learned head of a comparatively new educational institution, with great resources ultimately behind it. This man was building it on a sure and splendid foundation, in the hope that countless generations of youth would have cause to be grateful for the sagacious energy he was expending in their behalf.

He had, Selwyn knew, the wanderlust to a large degree, and the millionaire wondered whether, when this useful educator's slender income was augmented by the generous annuity he had planned to give him, he would continue his beneficent work or become a dweller in arabs' tents.

In the plenitude of his wealth and generosity, he had another in mind to share his largess. He was the orphaned son of an old and valued friend. He had helped the lad over some rough places, but had been careful not to do enough to slacken the boy's own endeavor. The young man had graduated from one of the best universities, and afterwards at a medical school that was worthy the name. He was, at the time Selwyn was planning the disposition of his wealth, about thirty years old, and was doing valuable laboratory work in one of the great research institutions. Gifted with superb health, and a keen analytical mind, he seemed to have it in him to go far in his profession, and perhaps be of untold benefit to mankind.

But Selwyn had noticed an indolent streak in the young scientist, and he wondered whether here again he was doing the fair and right thing by placing it within his power to lead a life of comparative ease and uselessness. Consequently, Selwyn moved cautiously in the matter of the distribution of his great wealth, and invoked Dru's aid. It was Dru's supernormal intellect, tireless energy, and splendid constructive ability that appealed to him, and he not only admired the Administrator above all men, but he had come to love him as a son. Dru was the only person with whom Selwyn had ever been in touch whose advice he valued above his own judgment. Therefore when the young Administrator suggested a definite plan of scientific giving, Selwyn gave it respectful attention at first, and afterwards his enthusiastic approval.

CHAPTER XLVII

The Wise Disposition of a Fortune, Continued

"IF YOUR fortune were mine, Senator Selwyn," said Philip Dru, "I would devote it to the uplift of women. Their full rights will be accorded them in time, but their cause could be accelerated by you, and meanwhile untold misery and unhappiness averted. Man, who is so dependent upon woman, has largely failed in his duty to her, not alone as an individual but as a sex. Laws are enacted, unions formed, and what not done for man's protection, but the working woman is generally ignored. With your money, and even more with your ability, you could change for the better the condition of girlhood and womanhood in every city and in every factory throughout the land. Largely because they are unorganized, women are overworked and underpaid to such an extent that other evils, which we deplore, follow as a natural sequence. By proper organization, by exciting public interest and enlisting the sympathy and active support of the humane element, which is to be found in every community you will be able to bring about better conditions.

"If I were you, I would start my crusade in New York and work out a model organization there, so that you could educate your coadjutors, as to the best methods, and then send them elsewhere to inaugurate the movement. Moreover, I would not confine my energies entirely to America, but Europe and other parts of the world should share its benefits, for human misery knows no sheltering land.

"In conjunction with this plan, I would carry along still another. Workingmen have their clubs, their societies and many places for social gathering, but the women in most cities have none. As you know, the great majority of working girls live in

217

tenements, crowded with their families in a room or two, or they live in cheap and lonely boarding houses. They have no chance for recreation after working hours or on holidays, unless they go to places it would be better to keep away from. If men wish to visit them, it must needs be in their bedrooms, on the street, or in some questionable resort."

"How am I to change this condition?" said Selwyn.

"In many ways," said Dru. "Have clubs for them, where they may sing, dance, read, exercise and have their friends visit them. Have good women in charge so that the influence will be of the best. Have occasional plays and entertainments for them, to which they may each invite a friend, and make such places pleasanter than others where they might go. And all the time protect them, and preferably in a way they are not conscious of. By careful attention to the reading matter, interesting stories should be selected each of which would bear its own moral. Quiet and informal talks by the matron and others at opportune times, would give them an insight into the pitfalls around them, and make it more difficult for the human vultures to accomplish their undoing. There is no greater stain upon our vaunted civilization," continued Dru, "than our failure to protect the weak, the unhappy and the abjectly poor of womankind.

"Philosophers still treat of it in the abstract, moralists speak of it now and then in an academic way, but it is a subject generally shunned and thought hopelessly impossible.

"It is only here and there that a big noble-hearted woman can be found to approach it, and then a Hull House is started, and under its sheltering roof unreckoned numbers of innocent hearted girls are saved to bless, at a later day, its patron saint.

"Start Hull Houses, Senator Selwyn, along with your other plan, for it is all of a kind, and works to the betterment of woman. The vicious, the evil minded and the mature sensual-ist, we will always have with us, but stretch out your mighty arm, buttressed as it is by fabulous wealth, and save from the lair of the libertines, the innocent, whose only crime is poverty and a hopeless despair.

"In your propaganda for good," continued Dru, "do not over-look the education of mothers to the importance of sex hygiene, so that they may impart to their daughters the truth, and not let them gather their knowledge from the streets.

"You may go into this great work, Senator Selwyn, with the consciousness that you are reaching a condition fraught with more consequence to society than any other that confronts it, for its ramifications for evil are beyond belief of any but the sociologist who has gone to its foundations."

CHAPTER XLVIII

An International Coalition

BUSY as General Dru had been rehabilitating domestic affairs, he never for a moment neglected the foreign situation. He felt that it was almost providential that he was in a position to handle it unhampered, for at no time in our history were we in such peril of powerful foreign coalition. Immediately after receiving from Selwyn the information concerning the British-German alliance, he had begun to build, as it were, a fire behind the British Ministry, and the result was its overthrow. When the English nation began to realize that a tentative agreement was being arrived at between their country on the one hand, and Germany and Japan on the other, with America as its object of attack, there was a storm of indignation; and when the new Ministry was installed the diplomatic machinery was set to work to undo, as nearly as could be, what their predecessors had accomplished.

In the meantime, Dru negotiated with them to the end that England and America were to join hands in a world wide policy of peace and commercial freedom. According to Dru's plan, disarmaments were to be made to an appreciable degree, custom barriers were to be torn down, zones of influence clearly defined, and an era of friendly commercial rivalry established.

It was agreed that America should approach Germany and Japan in furtherance of this plan, and when their consent was obtained, the rest would follow.

Dru worked along these lines with both nations, using consummate tact and skill. Both Germany and Japan were offended at the English change of front, and were ready to listen to other proposals. To them, he opened up a wide visit of commercial and territorial expansion, or at least its equivalent. Germany was to have the freest commercial access to South America, and she was invited to develop those countries both with German colonists and German capital.

There was to be no coercion of the governments, or political control in that territory, but on the other hand, the United States undertook that there should be no laws enacted by them to restrain trade, and that the rights of foreigners should have the fullest protection. Dru also undertook the responsibility of promising that there should be no favoritism shown by the South and Central American governments, but that native and alien should stand alike before the law so far as property rights were concerned.

Germany was to have a freer hand in the countries lying southeast of her and in Asia Minor. It was not intended that she should absorb them or infringe upon the rights as nations, but her sphere of influence was to be extended over them much the same as ours was over South America.

While England was not to be restricted in her trade relations with those countries, still she was neither to encourage emigration there nor induce capital to exploit their resources.

Africa and her own colonies were to be her special fields of endeavor.

In consideration of the United States lifting practically all custom barriers, and agreeing to keep out of the Eastern Hemisphere, upholding with her the peace and commercial freedom of the world, and of the United States recognizing the necessity of her supremacy on the seas, England, after having obtained the consent of Canada, agreed to relinquish her own sphere of political influence over the Dominion, and let her come under that of the United States. Canada was willing that this situation should be brought about, for her trade conditions had become interwoven with those of the United States, and the people of the two countries freely intermingled. Besides, since Dru had reconstructed the laws and constitution of the big republic, they were more in harmony with the Canadian institutions than before.

Except that the United States were not to appoint a Governor General, the republic's relations with Canada were to be much the same as those between herself and the Mother Country. The American flag, the American destiny and hers were to be interwoven through the coming ages.

In relinquishing this most perfect jewel in her Imperial crown, England suffered no financial loss, for Canada had long ceased to be a source of revenue, and under the new order of things, the trade relations between the two would be increased rather than diminished. The only wrench was the parting with so splendid a province, throughout which, that noble insignia of British supremacy, the cross of St. George, would be forever furled.

Administrator Dru's negotiations with Japan were no less successful than those with England. He first established cordial relations with her by announcing the intention of the United States to give the Philippines their independence under the protection of Japan, reserving for America and the rest of the world the freest of trade relations with the Islands.

Japan and China were to have all Eastern Asia as their sphere of influence, and if it pleased them to drive Russia back into Europe, no one would interfere.

That great giant had not yet discarded the ways and habits of mediævalism. Her people were not being educated, and she indicated no intention of preparing them for the responsibilities of self government, to which they were entitled. Sometimes in his day dreams, Dru thought of Russia in its vastness, of the ignorance and hopeless outlook of the people, and wondered when her deliverance would come. There was, he knew, great work for someone to do in that despotic land.

Thus Dru had formulated and put in motion an international policy, which, if adhered to in good faith, would bring about the comity of nations, a lasting and beneficent peace, and the acceptance of the principle of the brotherhood of man.

CHAPTER XLIX

Uneven Odds

GLORIA and Janet Selwyn saw much of one another in Washington, and Dru was with them both during those hours he felt necessary for recreation. Janet was ever bubbling over with fun and unrestrained humor, and was a constant delight to both Gloria and Dru. Somewhere deep in her soul there was a serious stratum, but it never came to the surface. Neither Gloria nor Dru knew what was passing in those turbulent depths, and neither knew the silent heartaches when she was alone and began to take an inventory of her innermost self. She had loved Dru from the moment she first saw him at her home in Philadelphia, but with that her prescience in such matters as only women have, she knew that nothing more than his friendship would ever be hers. She sometimes felt the bitterness of woman's position in such situations. If Dru had loved her, he would have been free to pay her court, and to do those things which oftentimes awaken a kindred feeling in another. But she was helpless. An advancement from her would but lessen his regard, and make impossible that which she most desired. She often wondered what there was between Gloria and Dru. Was there an attachment, an understanding, or was it one of those platonic friendships created by common interests and a common purpose? She wished she knew. She was reasonably sure of Gloria. That she loved Dru seemed to admit of little doubt. But what of him? Did he love Gloria, or did his love encompass the earth, and was mankind ever to be his wife and mistress? She wished she knew. How imperturbable he was! Was he to live and die a fathomless mystery? If he could not be hers, her generous heart plead for Gloria. She and Gloria often talked

225

of Dru. There was no fencing between these two. Open and enthusiastic admiration of Philip each expressed, but there were no confidences which revealed their hearts. Realizing that her love would never be reciprocated, Janet misled Philip as to her real feelings. One day when the three were together, she said, "Mr. Administrator, why don't you marry? It would add enormously to your popularity and it would keep a lot of us girls from being old maids." "How would it prevent your being an old maid, Janet?" said Dru. "Please explain." "Why, there are a lot of us that hope to have you call some afternoon, and ask us to be Mrs. Dru, and it begins to look to me as if some of us would be disappointed." Dru laughed and told her not to give up hope. And then he said more seriously — "Some day when my work here is done, I shall take your advice if I can find someone who will marry me." "If you wait too long, Philip, you will be so old, no one will want you," said Janet. "I have a feeling, Janet, that somewhere there is a woman who knows and will wait. If I am wrong, then the future holds for me many bitter and unhappy hours." Dru said this with such deep feeling that both Gloria and Janet were surprised. And Janet wondered whether this was a message to some unknown woman, or was it meant for Gloria? She wished she knew.

CHAPTER L

The Broadening of the Monroe Doctrine

IN SPITE of repeated warnings from the United States, Mexico and the Central American Republics had obstinately continued their old time habit of revolutions without just cause, with the result that they neither had stable governments within themselves, nor any hope of peace with each other.

One revolution followed another in quick succession, until neither life nor property was safe. England, Germany and other nations who had citizens and investments there had long protested to the American Government, and Dru knew that one of the purposes of the proposed coalition against the United States had been the assumption of control themselves.

Consequently, he took active and drastic steps to bring order out of chaos. He had threatened many times to police these countries, and he finally prepared to do so.

Other affairs of the Dru administration were running smoothly. The Army was at a high standard of efficiency, and the country was fully ready for the step when Dru sent one hundred thousand men to the Rio Grande, and demanded that the American troops be permitted to cross over and subdue the revolutionists and marauding bandits.

The answer was a coalition of all the opposing factions and the massing of a large army of defense. The Central American Republics also joined Mexico, and hurriedly sent troops north.

General Dru took personal command of the American forces, crossed the Rio Grande at Laredo, and war was declared. There were a large number of Mexican soldiers at Monterey, but they fell back in order to get in touch with the main army below Saltillo.

General Dru marched steadily on, but before he came to Saltillo, President Benevides, who commanded his own army, moved southward, in order to give the Central American troops time to reach him. This was accomplished about fifty miles north of the City of Mexico. The allies had one hundred thousand men, and the American force numbered sixty thousand, Dru having left forty thousand at Laredo, Monterey and Saltillo.

The two armies confronted one another for five days, General Benevides waiting for the Americans to attack, while General Dru was merely resting his troops and preparing them for battle. In the meantime, he requested a conference with the Mexican Commander, and the two met with their staffs midway between the opposing armies.

General Dru urged an immediate surrender, and fully explained his plans for occupation, so that it might be known that there was to be no oppression. He pointed out that it had become no longer possible for the United States to ignore the disorder that prevailed in Mexico and those countries south of it, for if the United States had not taken action, Europe would have done so. He expressed regret that a country so favored by God should be so abused by man, for with peace, order and a just administration of the government, Mexico and her sister republics, he felt sure, would take a high place in the esteem of the world. He also said that he had carefully investigated conditions, knew where the trouble lay, and felt sure that the mass of people would welcome a change from the unbearable existing conditions. The country was then, and had been for centuries, wrongfully governed by a bureaucracy, and he declared his belief that the Mexican people as a whole believed that the Americans would give them a greater measure of freedom and protection than they had ever known before.

Dru further told General Benevides that his army represented about all there was of opposition to America's offer of order and liberty, and he asked him to accept the inevitable, and not sacrifice the lives of the brave men in both commands.

Benevides heard him with cold but polite silence.

"You do not understand us, Senor Dru, nor that which we represent. We would rather die or be driven into exile than permit you to arrange our internal affairs as you suggest. There are a few families who have ruled Mexico since the first Spanish occupation, and we will not relinquish our hold until compelled to do so. At times a Juarez or a Diaz has attained to the Presidency, but we, the great families, have been the power behind each administration. The peons and canaille that you would educate and make our political equals, are now where they rightfully belong, and your endeavors in their behalf are misplaced and can have no result except disaster to them. Your great Lincoln emancipated many millions of blacks, and they were afterwards given the franchise and equal rights. But can they exercise that franchise, and have they equal rights? You know they have not. You have placed them in a worse position than they were before. You have opened a door of hope that the laws of nature forbid them to enter. So it would be here. Your theories and your high flown sentiment do you great credit, but, illustrious Senor, read the pages of your own history, and do not try to make the same mistake again. Many centuries ago the all knowing Christ advised the plucking of the mote from thine own eye before attempting to remove it from that of thy brother."

To this Dru replied: "Your criticism of us is only partly just. We lifted the yoke from the black man's neck, but we went too fast in our zeal for his welfare. However, we have taken him out of a boundless swamp where under the old conditions he must have wandered for all time without hope, and we have placed his feet upon firm ground, and are leading him with helping hands along the road of opportunity.

"That, though, Mr. President, is only a part of our mission to you. Our citizens and those of other countries have placed in your Republic vast sums for its development, trusting to your treaty guarantees, and they feel much concern over their inability to operate their properties, not only to the advantage of your people, but to those to whom they belong. We of Western Europe and the United States have our own theories as to the functions of government, theories that perhaps you fail to appreciate, but we feel we must not only observe them ourselves, but try and persuade others to do likewise.

"One of these ideas is the maintenance of order, so that when our hospitable neighbors visit us, they may feel as to their persons and property, as safe as if they were at home.

"I am afraid our views are wide apart," concluded Dru, "and I say it with deep regret, for I wish we might arrive at an understanding without a clash at arms. I assure you that my visit to you is not selfish; it is not to acquire territory or for the aggrandizement of either myself or my country, but it is to do the work that we feel must be done, and which you refuse to do."

"Senor Dru," answered Benevides, "it has been a pleasure to meet you and discuss the ethics of government, but even were I willing to listen to your proposals, my army and adherents would not, so there is nothing we can do except to finish our argument upon the field of battle."

The interview was therefore fruitless, but Dru felt that he had done his duty, and he prepared for the morrow's conflict with a less heavy heart.

CHAPTER LI

The Battle of La Tuna

IN THE numbers engaged, in the duration and in the loss of life, the battle of La Tuna was not important, but its effect upon Mexico and the Central American Republics was epoch making.

The manner of attack was characteristic of Dru's methods. His interview with General Benevides had ended at noon, and word soon ran through the camp that peace negotiations had failed with the result that the army was immediately on the alert and eager for action. Dru did not attempt to stop the rumor that the engagement would occur at dawn the next day. By dusk every man was in readiness, but they did not have to wait until morning, for as soon as supper was eaten, to the surprise of everyone, word came to make ready for action and march upon the enemy. Of Dru's sixty thousand men, twenty thousand were cavalry, and these he sent to attack the Mexican rear. They were ordered to move quietly so as to get as near to the enemy as possible before being discovered.

It was not long before the Mexican outposts heard the marching of men and the rumble of gun carriages. This was reported to General Benevides and he rode rapidly to his front. A general engagement at nightfall was so unusual that he could not believe the movement meant anything more than General Dru's intention to draw nearer, so that he could attack in the morning at closer range.

It was a clear starlight night, and with the aid of his glasses he could see the dark line coming steadily on. He was almost in a state of panic when he realized that a general attack was intended. He rode back through his lines giving orders in an excited and irregular way. There was hurry and confusion everywhere, and he found it difficult to get his soldiers to understand that a battle was imminent. Those in front were looking with a feeling akin to awe at that solid dark line that was ever coming nearer. The Mexicans soon began to fire from behind the breastworks that had been hastily erected during the few days the armies had been facing one another, but the shots went wild, doing but slight damage in the American ranks. Then came the order from Dru to charge, and with it came the Yankee yell. It was indeed no battle at all. By the time the Americans reached the earthworks, the Mexicans were in flight, and when the cavalry began charging the rear, the rout was completed.

In the battle of La Tuna, General Benevides proved himself worthy of his lineage. No general could have done more to rally his troops, or have been more indifferent to danger. He scorned to turn his back upon an enemy, and while trying to rally his scattered forces, he was captured, badly wounded.

Every attention worthy his position was shown the wounded man. Proud and chivalrous as any of his race, he was deeply humiliated at the miserable failure that had been made to repel the invaders of his country, though keenly touched by the consideration and courtesy shown him by the American General.

Dru made no spectacular entrance into the city, but remained outside and sent one of his staff with a sufficient force to maintain order. In an address announcing his intentions towards Mexico and her allies, Dru said — "It is not our purpose to annex your country or any part of it, nor shall we demand any indemnity as the result of victory further than the payment of the actual cost of the war and the maintenance of the American troops while order is being restored. But in the future, our flag is to be your flag, and you are to be directly under the protection of the United States. It is our purpose to give to your people the benefits of the most enlightened educational system, so that they may become fitted for the responsibilities of self-government. There will also be an equitable plan worked out by which the land now owned by a few will be owned by the many. In another generation, this beautiful land will be teeming with an educated, prosperous and contented people, who will regard the battlefield of La Tuna as the birthplace of their redemption.

"Above all things, there shall not be thrust upon the Mexican people a carpet-bag government. Citizens of Mexico are to enforce the reconstructed constitution and laws, and maintain order with native troops, although under the protecting arm of the United States.

"All custom duties are to be abolished excepting those uniform tariffs that the nations of the world have agreed upon for revenue purposes, and which in no way restrict the freedom of trade. It is our further purpose to have a constitution prepared under the direction and advice of your most patriotic and wisest men, and which, while modern to the last degree, will conform to your habits and customs.

"However," he said in conclusion, "it is our purpose to take the most drastic measures against revolutionists, bandits and other disturbers of the peace."

While Dru did not then indicate it, he had in mind the amalgamation of Mexico and the Central American Republics into one government, even though separate states were maintained.

CHAPTER LII

The Unity of the Northern Half of the Western Hemisphere Under the New Republic

SEVEN years had passed since Philip Dru had assumed the administration of the Republic. Seven years of serious work and heavy responsibility. His tenure of power was about to close, to close amidst the plaudits of a triumphant democracy. A Congress and a President had just been elected, and they were soon to assume the functions of government. For four years the States had been running along smoothly and happily under their new constitutions and laws. The courts as modified and adjusted were meeting every expectation, and had justified the change. The revenues, under the new system of taxation, were ample, the taxes were not oppressive, and the people had quickly learned the value of knowing how much and for what they were paying. This, perhaps, more than any other thing, had awakened their interest in public affairs.

The governments, both state and national, were being administered by able, well-paid men who were spurred by the sense of responsibility, and by the knowledge that their constituents were alert and keenly interested in the result of their endeavors.

Some of the recommendations of the many commissions had been modified and others adjusted to suit local conditions, but as a whole there was a general uniformity of statutes throughout the Union, and there was no conflict of laws between the states and the general government.

By negotiations, by purchase and by allowing other powers ample coaling stations along the Atlantic and Pacific coasts, the Bahamas, Bermuda and the British, French and Danish

West Indies were under American protection, and "Old Glory" was the undisputed emblem of authority in the northern half of the Western Hemisphere.

Foreign and domestic affairs were in so satisfactory a condition that the army had been reduced to two hundred thousand men, and these were broadly scattered from the Arctic Sea to the Canal at Panama. Since the flag was so widely flung, that number was fixed as the minimum to be maintained. In reducing the army, Dru had shown his confidence in the loyalty of the people to him and their satisfaction with the government given them.

Quickened by non-restrictive laws, the Merchant Marine of the United States had increased by leaps and bounds, until its tonnage was sufficient for its own carrying trade and a part of that of other countries.

The American Navy at the close of Philip Dru's wise administration was second only to that of England, and together the two great English speaking nations held in their keeping the peace and commercial freedom of the Seven Seas.

CHAPTER LIII

The Effacement of Philip Dru

IN THE years since he had graduated from West Point General Dru had learned to speak German, French and Spanish fluently, and he was learning with Gloria the language of the Slavs at odd moments during the closing months of his administration. Gloria wondered why he was so intent upon learning this language, and why he wanted her also to know it, but she no longer questioned him, for experience had taught her that he would tell her when he was ready for her to know.

His labors were materially lightened in these closing months, and as the time for his retirement drew near, he saw more and more of Gloria. Discarding the conventions, they took long rides together, and more frequently they took a few camp utensils, and cooked their mid-day meal in the woods. How glad Gloria was to see the pleasure these excursions gave him! No man of his age, perhaps of any age, she thought, had ever been under the strain of so heavy a responsibility, or had acquitted himself so well. She, who knew him best, had never seen him shirk his duty, nor try to lay his own responsibilities upon another's shoulders. In the hours of peril to himself and to his cause he had never faltered. When there was a miscarriage of his orders or his plans, no word of blame came from him if the effort was loyal and the unhappy agent had given all of his energy and ability.

He had met every situation with the fortitude that knows no fear, and with a wisdom that would cause him to be remembered as long as history lasts.

And now his life's work was done. How happy she was! If he did not love her, she knew he loved no one else, for never had she known him to be more than politely pleasant to other women.

One golden autumn day, they motored far into the hills to the west of Washington. They camped upon a mighty cliff towering high above the Potomac. What pleasure they had preparing their simple meal! It was hard for Gloria to realize that this lighthearted boy was the serious statesman and soldier of yesterday. When they had finished they sat in the warm sunshine on the cliff's edge. The gleaming river following its devious course far below them, parting the wooded hills in the distance. The evening of the year had come, and forest and field had been touched by the Master's hand. For a long time they sat silent under the spell that nature had thrown around them.

"I find it essential for the country's good to leave it for awhile, perhaps forever," said Philip Dru. "Already a large majority of the newly elected House have asked me to become the Executive. If I accepted, there would be those who would believe that in a little while, I would again assume autocratic control. I would be a constant menace to my country if I remained within it.

"I have given to the people the best service of which I was capable, and they know and appreciate it. Now I can serve them again by freeing them from the shadow of my presence and my name. I shall go to some obscure portion of the world where I cannot be found and importuned to return.

"There is at San Francisco a queenly sailing craft, manned and provisioned for a long voyage. She is waiting to carry me to the world's end if needs be."

Then Philip took Gloria's unresisting hand, and said, "My beloved, will you come with me in my exile? I have loved you since the day that you came into my life, and you can never know how I have longed for the hour to come when I would be able to tell you so. Come with me, dear heart, into this un-known land and make it glad for me. Come because I am drunken with love of you and cannot go alone. Come so that the days may be flooded with joy and at night the stars may sing to me because you are there. Come, sweet Gloria, come with me."

Happy Gloria! Happy Philip! She did not answer him. What need was there? How long they sat neither knew, but the sun was far in the west and was sending its crimson tide over an enchanted land when the lovers came back to earth.

Far out upon the waters of San Francisco Bay lay the grace-ful yet sturdy *Eaglet*. The wind had freshened, the sails were filled, and she was going swift as a gull through the Golden Gate into a shimmering sea.

A multitude of friends, and those that wished them well, had gathered on the water front and upon the surrounding hills to bid farewell to Philip Dru and his bride Gloria.

They watched in silent sadness as long as they could see the ship's silhouette against the western sky, and until it faded into the splendid waste of the Pacific.

Where were they bound? Would they return? These were the questions asked by all, but to which none could give answer.

THE END

What Co-partnership Can Do

BY EARL GREY
(Governor-General of Canada, 1904-11.)

One of the ablest champions of Co-partnership as a solution of the industrial problem is Earl Grey.

Below are some remarkable passages from his presidential address to the Labor Co-partnership Association.

THE problem before us is how to organize our industry on lines the fairness of which will be generally admitted. Fairplay is the keynote of our British character, and I am satisfied, if employers and employed are properly approached, that wherever a feeling of mutual sympathetic regard exists between them they will both be prepared to consider fairly and to meet fully each other's requirements. This is the belief on which we build our hopes of the future greatness of this country. Remove this belief and the outlook is one of blackest gloom.

Now what is the cause of the wide feeling of labor unrest? At the same time, while the average standard of living, as a result of better education, has been considerably raised and the retail prices of food have risen 9.3 per cent. since 1900, wages in that period have only risen 3 per cent. Consequently the manual workers find themselves in straitened, pinched, and most distressing circumstances. Their difficulties have naturally given birth to a general belief, or at any rate added strength to it, that they are not receiving their fair share of the wealth their labor has helped so largely to create. Now, whether this belief is justified or not, there can be no doubt of its existence.

241

LABOR AND CAPITAL IN OPPOSING CAMPS

The great fact with which we are confronted in the industries of to-day is that labor and capital are organized not in one but in opposing camps, with the object not so much of promoting the common well-being of all connected with industry as of securing whatever advantage can be obtained in the prosecution of their common industry for themselves. The members of each camp consequently regard each other with distrust and suspicion. The capitalist is inclined to give the minimum that is necessary to secure the labor which he requires, and the worker in return considers that all that should be required from him is the minimum of labor which will save him from dismissal.

Then not only have we to consider the limiting effect on the efficiency of industry caused by the fact that capital and labor are ranged not in one but in opposing camps, but we have also to consider the effect on the attitude of the men towards the management caused by the growing tendency of the small business to be swallowed up by the large combine. In such cases the old feeling of mutual affection, confidence, and esteem, which in the past bound together employer and employed, has been destroyed, and it must be obvious that unless we can adopt methods which will restore in a new, and perhaps in a more satisfactory manner, the old spirit the efficiency of industry and the prosperity of the nation will both suffer.

If you alter one part of any bit of machinery you must readjust all the other parts in order to secure smooth working, and if by substituting big businesses for small businesses you destroy the old intimate connection which formerly existed between masters and men, it would appear to be necessary, if you wish to maintain the old friendly relations between employer and employed, that you should establish your business on lines which will automatically create a feeling of loyalty on the part of all concerned to the industry with which they are connected.

How is that to be done? By co-partnership.

Now, what is the ideal of co-partnership?

Ideal co-partnership is a system under which worker and consumer shall share with capitalists in the profits of industry.

THE SURPLUS PROFITS GO TO CAPITAL

Under our present system the whole of the surplus profits go to capital, and it is the object of capital to give the worker the least wage for which he will consent to work, and to charge the consumer the highest price which he can be persuaded to give; conversely it is the object of labor to give as little as possible for the wage received.

Now, that is a system which cannot possibly satisfy the requirements of a civilized and well-organized society. What we want is a system which will safeguard the consumer, and also provide the worker with a natural, self-compelling inducement to help the industry with which he is connected. That system is provided by co-partnership. Co-partnership insists that the workers have a right to participate in the net profits that may remain after capital has received its fixed reward. In a co-partnership business, just as the reward of labor is fixed by the trade union rate of wages, so the reward of capital is fixed by the amount which it is necessary for the industry to give. That amount will vary corresponding with the security of the risk attending the industry in question. If the industry is a safe one, it will be able to obtain the capital required by giving a small interest; if the industry is a risky one, it will be necessary to offer capital better terms.

Then, if there should be surplus profits available for division after labor has received its fixed reward — viz., trade union rate of wages — and after capital has received its fixed reward — viz., the rate of interest agreed upon as the fair remuneration of capital; I say if, after these two initial charges have been met, there should still be left surplus profits to distribute, that instead of their going exclusively to capital they should be distributed between labor and capital on some principle of equity.

The way in which the principle of co-partnership can be supplied to industrial enterprise admits of infinite variety. In some cases the surplus profits are divided between wages, interest, and custom, in some cases between wages and custom without any share going to interest, and on some cases between wages and interest.

As an example of a co-partnership industry which divides all surplus profits that may remain after 5 per cent. has been paid on capital between custom and labor, one pound of purchase counting for as much in the division as one pound of wage, let me refer to the well-known Hebden Bridge Fustian Works. I commend to all interested in co-partnership questions a close study of this industry. Started by working men in 1870, it has built up on lines of permanent success a flourishing business, and is making sufficient profits to enable it to divide 9d. in the pound on trade union rate of wages and the same amount on purchases. The steady progress of this manufacturing industry over a period of forty-two years; the recognition by trade unionist management of the right of capital to receive an annual dividend of 5 per cent., and the resolute way in which they have written down the capital of £44,300 invested in land, buildings and machinery to £14,800, notwithstanding that a less conservative policy would have increased the sum available for bonus to wages, all go to show how practicable are co-partnership principles when they are applied by all concerned to productive enterprise in the right spirit.

A BRILLIANT EXAMPLE

I should also like to refer to Mr. Thompson's woolen mills of Huddersfield, established in 1886, as another brilliant example of successful co-partnership. It is frequently stated that in an industry where men are paid by piecework or share in the profits there is a tendency for the men to over-exert themselves. Well, in the Thompson Huddersfield mills there is no piecework, no overtime, only the weekly wage; no driving is allowed. The hours of labor are limited to forty-eight per week. The workers are given a whole week's holiday in August, and in addition they enjoy the benefits of a non-contributory sick and accident fund, and of a 24s. per week pension fund. In these mills cloth is made from wool and wool only, not an ounce of shoddy. Here again the surplus profits, after the fixed reward of capital — viz., interest at the rate of 5 per cent. per annum — has been paid, are divided between labor and custom; and here again the capital sunk in the mills has been written down from £8,655 to £1,680. Unprofitable machinery is scrap-heaped. The mill has only the best, most up-to-date machinery, and all connected with the works, shareholders and workers, live together like a happy family.

As an illustration of a co-partnership industry which divides its surplus profits between wages, interest, and custom, I might point to the gas companies which are being administered on the Livesey principle, which is now so well known. Since co-partnership principles were applied to the South Metropolitan Gas Works in 1899 over £500,000 has been paid, as their share of the profits, to the credit of the workers, who also own over £400,000 of the company's stock. The fact that over

£50,000,000 of capital is invested in gas companies administered on co-partnership principles, which divide surplus profits between consumers, shareholders, and wage-earners, encourages us to hope that we may look forward with confidence to the adoption of co-partnership principles by other industries.

As an illustration of a co-partnership industry which divides its surplus profits between labor and capital alone, let me refer to the Walsall Padlock Society, one of the 114 workmen productive societies which may be regarded as so many different schools of co-partnership under exclusive trade unionist management. In this society the rate of interest on share capital has been fixed at $7^1/2$ per cent., and should there be any surplus profit after trade union rate of wages and the fixed reward of capital, $7^1/2$ per cent., have been paid, it is divided between labor and capital in proportion to the value of their respective services, and the measure of the value is the price the Walsall Padlock Society pays for the use of capital and labor respectively. £1 of interest counts for as much in the division of the profits as £1 of wage, and vice versa. This principle of division, invented by the Frenchman Godin, of Guise, has always seemed to me to be absolutely fair and to be capable of being easily applied to many industries.

Now in these cases I have quoted, and I could refer to many others, a unity of interest is established between labor and capital, with the result that there is a general atmosphere of peace and of mutual brotherhood and goodwill.

Capital receives the advantage of greater security. Labor is secured the highest rate of wage the industry can afford.

WILLING AND UNWILLING SERVICE

Now, what does the substitution of such conditions for the

conditions generally prevailing to-day in England mean for our country? Who shall estimate the difference between the value of willing and unwilling service? The Board of Trade will tell you that a man paid by piecework is generally from 30 to 50 per cent. more effective than a man paid by time.

If the co-partnership principle, which is better than piece-work, because it tends to produce identity of interest between capital and labor were to increase the efficiency of time-paid workers from 30 to 50 per cent., just think of the result; and yet the fact that co-partnership might add from 30 to 50 per cent. to the efficiency of the worker is urged by many trade unionists as a reason against co-partnership. They seem to fear that the result of making men co-partners will be to cause them to give 25 per cent. better labor and to receive only 50 per cent. more wage. No system can be right which is based on the assumption that self-interest calls for a man to give his worst instead of his best. When I compare Canada with England I am struck by the fact, that, whereas Canada's greatest undeveloped asset is her natural resources, England's greatest undeveloped asset is man himself. How to get each man to do his best is the problem before England to-day. It is because co-partnership harnesses to industry not only the muscle but the heart and the intelligence of the worker that we are justified in regarding it with reverence and enthusiasm as the principle of the future.

APPENDIX

Page 191. Sub. 1. Par. 2.

The former qualification was five years' residence in the United States and in many States there were no restrictions placed upon education, nor was an understanding of the English language necessary.

Page 191. Sub. 1. Par. 3.

Dru saw no good reason for limiting the time when an exceptionally endowed man could begin to serve the public.

Page 191. Sub. 1. Par. 4.

The Senate under Dru's plan of Government becomes a quasi-judicial body, and it was his purpose to prevent any member of it or of the regular judiciary from making decisions with a view of furthering their political fortunes. Dru believed that it would be of enormous advantage to the Nation if Judges and Senators were placed in a position where their motives could not be questioned and where their only incentive was the general welfare.

Page 192. Sub. 2. Par. 1.

Why deprive the Republic of the services of a useful man because his particular district has more good congressional timber than can be used and another district has none? Or again, why relegate to private life a man of National importance merely because his residence happens to be in a district not entirely in harmony with his views?

Page 192. Par. 2.

The recall is here used for the reason that the term has been extended six years, though the electorate retains the privilege of dismissing an undesirable member at the end of every two years.

Page 192. Par. 3.

The purpose here was to convene the House within two months instead of thirteen months after its election, and to limit its size in order to promote efficiency.

Page 193. Sub. 3. Par. 1.

The reason for using the recall here is that the term is lengthened to life and it seemed best to give the people a right to pass upon their Senators at stated periods.

Page 198. Sub. 3 Par. 1b.

The recall is used here, as in other instances, because of the lengthened term and the desirability of permitting the people to pass upon a Governor's usefulness at shorter periods.

Introduction to the Appendices

The following primary source documents have been appended to this novel to illustrate the historical significance of the novel and its author's impact on American public policy. The first three items are taken from *The Intimate Papers of Colonel House*, a four-volume series published in two volumes each in both 1926 and 1928. *The Intimate Papers* was edited and written by Charles Seymour, the Yale historian chosen by House to prepare the papers for partial publication. That House approved of the result of Seymour's work, there is no doubt. House himself wrote a "Prefatory Note" for publication in the first volume. Seymour published the papers, along with his own narrative, just three and a half years after House donated most of his papers to the Yale University Library in 1922.

The final appendix is a letter of explanation House wrote from France on his purpose in composing *Philip Dru*. The original of the typed letter is stored in the E.M. House Papers of Yale University Library, where most of House's papers remain — largely ignored — to this day.

Appendix One

The Significance of *Philip Dru*

The following essay by Col. House's biographer, Yale University Historian Charles Seymour, explains how Philip Dru *relates to House's personal beliefs. The material is reproduced from Volume One of* The Intimate Papers of Colonel House *(Boston and New York: Houghton Mifflin, 1926), pp. 152-158).*

The extent of Colonel House's influence upon the legislative plans of the Administration may be gathered from a remarkable document which deserves some attention. In the autumn of 1912, immediately after the presidential election, there was published a novel, or political romance, entitled 'Philip Dru: Administrator.' It was the story of a young West Point graduate, incapacitated for military service by his health, who was caught by the spirit of revolt against the tyranny of privileged interests. A stupid and reactionary Government at Washington provokes armed rebellion, in which Dru joins wholeheartedly and which he ultimately leads to complete success. He himself becomes dictator and proceeds by ordinance to remake the mechanism of government, to reform the basic laws that determine the relation of the classes, to remodel the defensive forces of the republic, and to bring about an international grouping or league of powers, founded upon Anglo-Saxon solidarity. His reforms accomplished, he gives effect once more to representative institutions as formulated in a new American Constitution, better fitted than the old for the spirit and conditions of the twentieth century.

As a romance, the book was not notable, for the effort of the anonymous author had evidently been spent upon the careful working-out of the political and social ideas of the young Philip Dru rather than upon its literary form. Certain reviewers, however, were piqued by the daring and the ingenuity of these ideas and, treating the book as a political manifesto rather than a novel, acclaimed it as a remarkable publication. Speculation as to the personality of the unknown author, who was described merely as 'a man prominent in political councils,' naturally followed. There seemed to be general agreement that he could not belong to either of the two older parties. 'We trust he is to be found among the Democrats,' wrote one reviewer, 'but we greatly fear he is of the New Party.' Another reviewer was of similar opinion: 'We trust that the author's counsel and assistance will be available at Washington, if not during the present Administration, surely when the Progressive Party assumes control.' There were, indeed, numerous suggestions that Mr. [Theodore] Roosevelt himself was the author.

Five years after its publication an enterprising bookseller, noting the growing influence of House in the Wilson Administration, wrote with regard to the book: 'As time goes on the interest in it becomes more intense, due to the fact that so many of the ideas expressed by "Philip Dru: Administrator," have become laws of this Republic, and so many of his ideas have been discussed as becoming laws.' And he ends with the question, 'Is Colonel E. M. House of Texas the author? If not, who is?'

Colonel House was, in truth, the author; to his other occupations he had added that of novelist. He tells us himself in a brief memorandum how, in the autumn of 1911, he conceived the idea of writing a novel as a medium to express his economic and political theories. That winter in Austin he was seriously ill.

'When I began to convalesce at home, and before I was able to get about, I wrote "Philip Dru: Administrator." I was surprised at the rapidity with which I wrote, for I was not certain when I began that I could do it at all....

'I was also surprised to find how much I was interested in doing this kind of work. I had written platforms, speeches, etc., for different candidates and officials, and newspaper articles for campaign purposes, but this was an entirely new departure. I did not spend more than thirty days upon the first draft of the book. Mezes read and approved it, and I sent it to Houston to look over, largely with the view of getting his judgment as to the economic features of it.

'He kept the manuscript until I passed through St. Louis on my way East. He declared his belief that it was economically sound, but held that the fiction in it was so thin that he advised rewriting it as a serious work, as he had suggested originally.'

Colonel House to Dr. D. F. Houston

AUSTIN, TEXAS, *March* 12, 1912

DEAR DOCTOR HOUSTON:

. . . I expect to elaborate somewhat concerning the functions of the National Government.

I particularly want to make it clear that the Executive and his Cabinet will be more nearly akin to the English Premier than to the French, inasmuch as I want him to have the right to propose measures directly and without referring them to a committee.

If you have any suggestions along this or any other lines, please let me have them.

I have done some padding—as, for instance, the story of

the tenement fire—which I expect to take out later and put in more serious stuff.

It is not much of a novel, as you will soon discover; at the same time, unless it were known by that name its audience would be reduced at least ninety-nine per cent. If it was called what I really mean it to be, only those who think pretty much as I do would read it, and those I am trying to reach would never look at it.

Faithfully yours,
E. M. HOUSE

But this was the spring of 1912, and all of House's energies were taken up with the pre-convention campaign that ended with the nomination of Wilson. The early summer he spent in Europe. Evidently not wishing to give the time necessary to putting it into the form that Mr. Houston advised, by elimination of the romance, and fearing that a scientific essay would not reach a large public, he decided merely to smooth it out so far as possible while on the Atlantic.

'I worked assiduously on "Philip Dru" all the way over and all the way back, but had no time for it in Europe.... We returned early in August, and the first thing I did was to shake myself clear of "Philip Dru."'

'E. S. Martin read the manuscript and wanted me to rewrite it, saying that "some of it was so good that it was a pity that parts of it were so bad." I had no time, however, for such diversions, for the political campaign was engrossing my entire time and the publisher was urging me to give him the manuscript so it might be advertised in the autumn announcements.

'I was so much more interested in the campaign than I was in the book that I turned it over to the publisher, having determined to let it go as it was.'

Whatever the literary merits of 'Philip Dru,' it gives us an insight into the main political and social principles that actuated House in his companionship with President Wilson.

Through it runs the note of social democracy reminiscent of Louis Blanc and the revolutionaries of 1848: 'This book is dedicated to the unhappy many who have lived and died lacking opportunity....' 'The time is now measurably near when it will be just as reprehensible for the mentally strong to hold in subjection the mentally weak, and to force them to bear the grievous burdens which a misconceived civilization has imposed upon them.' Government, accordingly, must be inspired by the spirit of charity rather than the spirit of ruthless efficiency. Especially must privileged interests be excluded from governmental influence, for by the nature of things their point of view is selfish.

Through the book also runs the idea that in the United States, government is unresponsive to popular desires—a 'negative' government, House calls it—for it is at more pains to do nothing with safety than to attempt desirable reforms which might disturb vested interests and alienate the voters. 'We have been living under a Government of negation.' The theory of checks and balances has developed so as to reinforce this negative character of government; closer cooperation between the President and Congress, perhaps in the direction of parliamentary methods, is necessary if the tendency of American government is to be made active and positive.

The specific measures enacted by Philip Dru as Administrator of the nation, indicated the reforms desired by House.

The Administrator appointed a 'board composed of economists and others well versed in matters relating to the tariff and internal revenue, who . . . were instructed to work out a tariff law which would contemplate the abolition of the theory of protection as a governmental policy.'

'The Administrator further directed the tax board to work out a graduated income tax....'

Philip Dru also provided for the 'formulation of a new banking law, affording a flexible currency bottomed largely upon commercial assets, the real wealth of the nation, instead of upon debt, as formerly.... Its final construction would completely destroy the credit trust, the greatest, the most far-reaching, and under evil direction the most pernicious trust of all.'

'He also proposed making corporations share with the Government and States a certain part of their net earnings....'

Such were some of Dru's plans which shortly found actual life in Wilsonian legislation. No wonder that Cabinet members like Mr. Lane and Mr. Bryan commented upon the influence of Dru with the President. 'All that book has said should be,' wrote Lane, 'comes about.... The President comes to "Philip Dru" in the end.'[1]

Other excerpts indicate the extent of House's progressiveness.

'Labor is no longer to be classed as an inert commodity to be bought and sold by the law of supply and demand.'

Dru 'prepared an old-age pension law and also a laborer's insurance law covering loss in cases of illness, incapacity, and death.'

'He had incorporated in the Franchise Law the right of Labor to have one representative upon the boards of corporations and to share a certain percentage of the earnings above the wages, after a reasonable per cent upon the capital had been earned. In turn it was to be obligatory upon them [the laborers] not to strike, but to submit all grievances to arbitration.'

To such an extent had Colonel House formulated his ideas upon national problems before the election of Wilson. 'In regard to "Philip Dru,"' wrote House in 1916, 'I want to say that there are some things in it I wrote hastily and in which I do not concur, but most of it I stand upon as being both my ethical and political faith.'

---

[1]Letters of Franklin K. Lane, p. 297.

Appendix Two

E.M. House's Influence on
President Wilson and Public Policy

The following essay by Col. House's biographer, Yale University Historian Charles Seymour, expounds on the depth of the relationship between E. M. House and President Wilson. The material is reproduced from Volume One of The Intimate Papers of Colonel House *(Boston and New York: Houghton Mifflin Company, 1926) pp. 114-118.*

CHAPTER V
THE SILENT PARTNER

The source of his power was . . . the confidence that men had in his sagacity and unselfishness.
E. S. Martin in 'Harper's Magazine,' February, 1912

I

'MR. HOUSE is my second personality. He is my independent self. His thoughts and mine are one. If I were in his place I would do just as he suggested.... If any one thinks he is reflecting my opinion by whatever action he takes, they are welcome to the conclusion.'

Such was the reply given by President Wilson to a politician who asked whether House represented him accurately in a certain situation. It indicates the degree of confidence which he placed in the Colonel. The President made it clear that, although House had refused official position of any kind, he was determined that the Administration should not lose the political services which House was qualified to perform. On the very day of his inauguration he asked and summarily accepted his recommendations for important appointive posts.

'The President-elect telephoned [Colonel House wrote on March 4] and asked Loulie and me to meet his family party at the Shoreham Hotel at 9.45, in order to accompany them to the Capitol for the inauguration ceremonies. I took Loulie to the Shoreham and left her with the Wilsons, but I did not go to the Capitol myself. I went instead to the Metropolitan Club and loafed around with Wallace. Functions of this sort do not appeal to me and I never go.

'Mrs. Wilson invited us to the White House to see the fireworks. When we arrived we found the President was over in his office. I went there and was with him for a few minutes in order to tell him that I had investigated John H. Marble for Interstate Commerce Commissioner, in place of F. K. Lane, and had found him satisfactory. The President had never met Marble and had made no inquiries concerning him further than mine. He said he would send his name in to-morrow, along with the names of his Cabinet. He made the appointment in this way in order to avoid the great pressure which would be made upon him by candidates for this important office....'

'March 8, 1913: The President asked me to be at the White House this morning at nine.

'The offices were nearly deserted at so early an hour. The President was dressed in a very becoming sack suit of grey, with a light grey silk tie. It was rather an informal-looking costume, but very attractive. I sat with him for nearly an hour and we had a delightful talk. We discussed the Cabinet mainly, and he laughingly told me his estimate of each one and how they acted at the first meeting.... The President spoke finely of Bryan and said their relations were exceedingly cordial.

'The President suggested that we could have a cypher between us, so when we talked over the telephone or wrote we could discuss men without fear of revealing their identity. He took a pencil and started out with Bryan, saying, "Let us call him 'Primus.'" McAdoo is already known as "Pythias,"

McCombs being "Damon." Garrison he suggested as "Mars," McReynolds "Coke," Burleson "Demosthenes."'

Thus began House's career as Silent Partner.[2] It was a relationship which rested chiefly upon the political coöperation of the Colonel in meeting the problems of government. His labors were of the most varied kind, and he sought every opportunity to ease the load that bore upon the President, to bring him information, to work out details of policy. There was, however, an essential personal basis to the relationship, since it would have been impossible for a man of Wilson's temperament to put full political confidence in a man who did not evoke his affection as an individual.

'I have an intimate personal matter to discuss with you [he said to House in the summer of 1915]. You are the only person in the world with whom I can discuss everything.[3] There are some I can tell one thing and others another, but you are the only one to whom I can make an entire clearance of mind.'

The letters of Wilson to House invariably displayed an intensity of personal feeling that would have astounded those who attributed to him about the same degree of warmth as that of a Euclidean proposition and failed to realize the human qualities that lay concealed under his armor of exterior austerity. He wrote him frequently of his desire to talk with him and the need and desire for his advice on many a complicated matter. At the end of the first legislative session, he put his feeling into emphatic language.

'Your letter on the passage of the Tariff Bill [the President said] gave me the kind of pleasure that seldom comes to a man, and it goes so deep that no words are adequate to express it. I

---

[2]The appellation was first used by Peter Clark Macfarlane in an article in *Collier's,* and soon became general.

[3]This was after Mrs. Wilson's death and before the President's remarriage.

think you must know without my putting it into words (for I cannot) how deep such friendship and support goes with me and how large a part it constitutes of such strength as I have in public affairs. I thank you with all my heart and with deep affection.'

The friendship between the two, however rapidly it bloomed, was progressive. It is not uninteresting and is perhaps significant to trace its development through the forms of salutation used by the President in his letters. They met in November, 1911, and until the following spring Wilson addresses him as 'Dear Mr. House.' But after his nomination, in August, 1912, he begins to address him as 'Dear Friend,' signing himself 'Faithfully yours,' or 'Sincerely yours.' After his election in November, 1912, he signs himself 'Affectionately yours,' and this is constant with the salutation of 'Dear Friend,' for two and a half years. In moments of great emotion, as at the time of Mrs. Wilson's death, he addresses him as 'My dear, dear Friend.' In the summer of 1915, at the period of the *Arabic* crisis when he was torn by doubt and worry, the President begins to address him as 'Dearest Friend,' a salutation which remains invariable until after his reëlection in November, 1916. In January of 1917 the President reverts to the form of address, 'My dear House,' although he continues the conclusion, 'Affectionately yours.' Otherwise it is impossible to detect in Wilson's letters any change of tone. It is certain that the political relationship between the two men remained as close during the two years that followed; but it is possible that their personal friendship was most intense between the years 1912 and 1917.

Close spiritual communion was not dependent upon physical propinquity, for the heat drove Colonel House far from Washington in the spring and frequently several months would pass without their meeting. Separation seems to have made no difference in their understanding. 'I never worry when I do not hear from you,' wrote House. 'No human agency could make me doubt your friendship and affection.... I always understand your motives.' At the end of each summer, enterprising and ill-informed newspapermen would regularly feature a 'break.' 'You are a little behind your schedule this year, my friend,' said House to a reporter one September day, after the publication of the annual story.

During the cool months, however, Wilson and House saw much of each other, for the latter made frequent trips to Washington, and on each of these trips Wilson devoted long hours to intimate discussions with his adviser. The President lacked the capacity and inclination for meeting and entertaining varied types of people which, under the Roosevelt régime, made the White House a magnet for explorers, littérateurs, pugilists, and hunters—every one who had an interesting story to tell. Wilson had the college professor's love of a quiet evening by the fireside with the family, and an early bed, varied by a visit to the theatre, preferably a simple vaudeville.

House was one of the few admitted to the small family circle. 'At night,' said Herbert Corey in the *Commercial Advertiser,* 'after Mr. Wilson had wound the clock, and put out the cats and politicians, House stayed for a little further talk.' To the President's study House brought the impressions he had formed of public opinion, gathered from his numerous contacts with office-holders, business men, and editors, and there Wilson gave free vent to his political theories, his aspirations, and his fears. There, too, the President found relaxation in reading poetry and essays to his friend.

Appendix Three
E.M. House's Role in Formation of the League of Nations Proposal

The following essay by Col. House's biographer, Yale University Historian Charles Seymour, explains part of the early and critical role House played in influencing Wilson to formulate a League of Nations-style proposal. The material is reproduced from Volume Two of The Intimate Papers of Colonel House *(Boston and New York: Houghton Mifflin Company, 1928, pp. 293-298).*

CHAPTER X
WAR NERVES

They get more and more on edge as the strain becomes severer. There'll soon be very few sane people left in the world.
Ambassador Page to House, June 2, 1916, from London

You cannot conceive of the general breakdown of nerves among this people.
Ambassador Gerard to House, August 30, 1916, from Berlin

I

By refusing the plan which Wilson had offered through House, the Allies postponed the advent of American aid to Europe for the best part of a year. The plan, however, was not without its historical importance, for it led President Wilson to crystallize his ideas as to America's rôle in world affairs and to announce publicly, on May 27, 1916, that henceforth the United States must take an active part in world politics. At the same time he advocated the creation of a League of Nations as the mainspring of a reorganized international system.

Wilson had been moving gradually in this direction during the two preceding years. He had cautiously approved House's Great Adventure of 1914, the purpose of which was to establish an understanding between Great Britain, Germany, and the United States in order to tide over the war crisis that threatened. He had accepted with enthusiasm the plan for the Pan-American Pact, which provided for a mutual guaranty of political independence and territorial integrity for all American States. At the beginning of 1916 he had cabled House, for the information of Grey and Balfour, that he was willing to enter a world pact of the same nature. Now he publicly announced the fact, extending to all the world the principles of the proposed Pan-American covenant.

Since the announcement would involve an obvious revolution in American foreign policy, the end of the traditional policy of isolation, House cast about for a suitable occasion upon which such a momentous step might be taken. 'It occurred to me,' he wrote on May 9, 'that the 27th of May, when the League to Enforce Peace meets in Washington, would be the right time to make this proposal, and I am so suggesting to the President. I have arranged with the Secretary of the League to have ex-President Taft, who is President of the League, send another invitation to the President.' The next day a letter from Mr. Taft to Colonel House brought the message inviting Wilson to make the chief speech.

It might have become an even more significant occasion than it proved to be, for as originally planned it was designed to serve a double purpose. In his speech the President would demand the calling of a conference that might end the war, at the same time that he laid down the principles upon which a durable peace must be based. Through all the speech was to run the thesis that henceforth the United States was ready to share with the other nations of the world the responsibilities of mankind for the maintenance of peace and justice.

The discouraging attitude assumed by the Allies, however, convinced Wilson and House that more harm than good would be accomplished by making the demand for an immediate conference. On the eve of delivery, accordingly, they decided to utilize the occasion simply for a general exposition of American foreign policy and American willingness to coöperate in an association of nations.

'We agreed [noted Colonel House on May 24, after a conference with Mr. Wilson] it would be wise in the circumstances to modify greatly the speech he is to make next Saturday before the League to Enforce Peace. He is to treat the subject as we have outlined it, with the exception that he is not to do more than hint at peace. He asked for a pad and made a memorandum. We divided the subject into four parts, and indicated just how far he should go.'

House recognized fully the extent of the revolution in American policy that was indicated by the terms and the implications of the address. For Wilson threw completely to one side the doctrine of isolation. 'We are participants,' said the President, 'whether we would or not, in the life of the world. The interests of all nations are our own also. We are partners with the rest. What affects mankind is inevitably our affair as well as the affair of the nations of Europe and of Asia.'

It was therefore with a full consciousness of the seriousness of the step about to be taken that the Colonel worked out the details of the speech with Mr. Wilson. He was confident that the President could capture the moral leadership of mankind through the decisive step he was taking — 'a decision,' House wrote, 'that marks the turning-point in our international relations and in our old-time non-interference policy.'

'I feel sure, if he will follow our present plans all the way through, history will give him one of the highest places among the statesmen of the world. It does not matter whether he mediates or not; but what does matter is for him to strike the high note, the right note, and hold to it regardless of consequences to himself. He can and will become the dominant factor in the situation, because he, of all the statesmen now living, is the only one in a position of power necessary to accomplish the task.'

On May 18 the President had written to House, thanking him for suggestions and asking for more. What would House say if he were going to make the speech and base it upon the understanding he had with Grey as to future guaranties of peace? Wilson asked also for a copy of a letter he had written him regarding those guaranties, indicating the rather surprising fact that the President did not keep copies of some of his most important letters.

Wilson obviously planned to use the Grey-House understanding as to guaranties as the groundwork of his speech, and to Grey Wilson was largely indebted for the basic idea that underlay his speech: that the World War would not have come if there had been some organized system by which nations could be brought in conference when the crisis arose. Colonel House, it is interesting to note, urged Wilson to avoid the advocacy of a complicated mechanism at this stage—such as the League to Enforce Peace put forward—and to confine himself to generalities until the nations accepted the idea of association. Then, as later in the contest with the Senate, House did not want the principle to be endangered by a dispute over details.

Colonel House to the President

NEW YORK, *May* 19, 1916

DEAR GOVERNOR:

I am sending you some data to look over which may be of service to you in formulating your speech.

Norman Angell gave me the quotations from the speeches of Asquith, Grey, Balfour, and others, and Bryce's article in *The New Republic* has a direct bearing upon the same subject.

My reason for thinking the programme of the League to Enforce Peace impracticable at this time is that I believe the first thing to do is to get the Governments to agree to stand together for the things which you have so admirably outlined in your letter to me and which I in substance cabled to Grey.[4]

When there is a committal upon these points, then the question of putting them into practical use will arise and some such tribunal as they suggest may he worked out....

As soon as you begin to discuss details, you will find differences arising that might obscure the real issue.

I shall write you further Sunday.

---

[4] A letter of May 16, in which Wilson summarizes his proposal in a sentence which, with slight alterations, became the chief sentence of his speech: 'An universal alliance to maintain freedom of the seas and to prevent any war begun either (*a*) contrary to treaty covenants or (*b*) without full warning and full inquiry—a virtual guaranty of territorial integrity and political independence.' (Quoted in Diary of Colonel House, May 17, 1916.) In the speech Wilson changed *alliance* to read *association of the nations; freedom of the seas* to read *the inviolate security of the highway of the seas for the common and unhindered use of all the nations of the world,* (in order to assure the British that the suggestion was not directed against their restrictions on trade as much as against the submarine); *full inquiry* to read *full submission of the causes to the opinion of the world.*

Affectionately yours
E. M. House

_____

New York, *May* 21, 1916

Dear Governor:

I am sending you my thoughts on the speech you have in hand. It is roughly and quickly done and is no more than a suggestion....

I hope you will show Lansing the speech before it is delivered. He might be useful and he would surely be offended if he did not know of this important step.

I am writing hastily but with deep affection.

Your devoted
E. M. House

The draft which Colonel House enclosed in his letter of May 21 is of historical interest because of the extent to which the President utilized it in the address of May 27, an address which sums up the gist of his international aims during the following years.[5] Wilson's later speeches were merely a refinement of details and a development of the ideas contained in this address.

Underlying the entire address ran the thought of the failure of diplomacy and the impotence of Europe as manifested in the outbreak and the prolongation of the war. A new system was essential to safeguard the principles which, Wilson insisted, must serve as the basis of international relations. Those principles he underlined carefully:

_____

[5]See Appendix to chapter, for a comparison of House's draft and the final text of Wilson's address.

'First, that every people has a right to choose the sovereignty under which they shall live....

'Second, that the small states of the world have a right to enjoy the same respect for their sovereignty and for their territorial integrity that great and powerful nations expect and insist upon.

'And, third, that the world has a right to be free from every disturbance of its peace that has its origin in aggression and disregard of the rights of peoples and nations.'

These were the principles which Wilson had already emphasized in his Mobile address, but he now carried his policy from a negative and abstract to a positive and concrete position, by indicating a definite mechanism to enforce them. In order to maintain those principles, international coöperation must be substituted for anarchy and conflict through 'an universal association of the nations to maintain the inviolate security of the highway of the seas for the common and unhindered use of all the nations of the world and to prevent any war begun either contrary to treaty covenants or without warning and full submission of the causes to the opinion of the world—a virtual guaranty of territorial integrity and political independence.' Thus was the verbiage of the Pan-American Pact extended to cover a projected world pact; it was to become of increasing importance, until, as Article X of the League of Nations covenant, it seemed to Wilson the heart of the entire settlement.

Appendix Four

E.M. House's Personal Explanation
of the Purpose of Philip Dru

Following is a heretofore unpublished letter by Edward Mandell House, explaining both his purpose in composing the novel and the extent to which the novel represents his beliefs. The original letter remains in the Edward Mandell House Papers, Manuscripts and Archives, Yale University Library, from which this is reprinted with permission.

Cabourg, Calvados, France
July 10, 1922

"Philip Dru" was written in December and January of 1911-12 at Austin, Texas, during the six weeks I was convalescing from a protracted illness.

It was my intention to re-write it during the summer of 1912, but when I returned to New York in April of that year I found myself submerged in the campaign being waged to nominate Governor Woodrow Wilson as the democratic candidate for President.

During a hurried trip to Russia that summer I had but scant time to go over the manuscript, and when I returned to America I again became engrossed in the national elections, and being pressed by the publishers, consented to its immediate publication anonymously. Early November of 1912 found it upon the book-stands, but it also found Woodrow Wilson President-elect of the United States, therefore, I have never had the leisure to read "Philip Dru" except in manuscript.

It was written in the form of fiction in the hope that it would reach a wider public in that guise, but when it was finished, I saw that the material of an economic and governmental character which I had put in it was far too heavy to carry any story, much less the one around which I had thrown it.

When I indicated my purpose to read and perhaps re-write the book I was advised to discard the fiction and put out the substance of it in a number of essarys [sic] on government. However, I have finally concluded to leave it as it is, and to write this word of explanation.

Governmental affairs, both domestic and foreign, have been almost my sole interest during and since boyhood. For a long time it had seemed to me that our Government was too complicated in its machinery and that we had outgrown our Constitution. It has been by constant wonder that our people were willing to go along without protest with such an inefficient machine.

When our Republic was conceived, there was no modern guide-post to point the right direction in which to go. France had overthrown one monarch only to accept another. Therefore it was to be expected that the makers of our Constitution should proceed with caution and place within it checks and balances.

The climate, the character of the population and, more than all, our great natural resources have caused us to move forward in the acquisition of wealth at phenonmeal [sic] speed, and this in itself has been sufficient to keep our people content.

When things are going well it is the part of wisdom to use care in making changes of any sort, and things have undeniably gone well with us up to the present. But we have taken many chances which were unnecessary, and still continue to take them. One of these chances has been the succession to the Presidency. If the crisis of 1876 had not followed so closely upon the Civil War, or if a man of different temperament than that of Samuel J. Tilden had been "counted out," there can be but little doubt that physical force would have been substituted for the milder measure of compromise which was adopted.

We hearkened to the warning sufficiently to change the method of procedure somewhat, but there is still much to be desired. It has never been settled whether the House, Senate or both concurrently shall count the vote and determine its validity. The makers of the Constitution contemplated an entirely different procedure from that now in use. In the early days Electors were voted for as now, but these, in turn, had the sole responsibility of choosing a President. Today an Elector is a mere automaton, and while he has the constitutional right to vote for whom he pleases, he would no more dare exercise it than the King of Great Britain would dare to use his right of veto.

Without entering into a discussion of whether the change which has come about is for the best, there should be no difference of opinion as to the advisability of adjusting the legal procedure to fit conditions as they are now rather than as they were a century and a half ago.

The partisan heat now engendered in the election of a President should in itself be a warning to us to change the procedure so there should never be a question as to its legality. And while doing so, some method determining the disability of a President should definitely be reached. If this is not done, a conjunction of circumstances may some day arise which may cause civil war.

These questions do not present any insoluable [sic] difficulties, and all that is necessary to take away the hazard of danger is for the President and Congress to clarify the law in order to meet the requirements of the situation.

The negative character of our Government and its lack of responsiveness to the will of the people makes it less efficient than it should be. No unprejudiced student of governmental affairs will question the assertion of Lord Bryce that "America is the most undemocratic of democratic countries". When he wrote this he probably had in mind Russia, Japan and Germany as being the only countries throughout the world less democratic than the United States.

One of the purposes in writing "Philip Dru" was a desire to bring to a [sic] our people a realization of this. We are pleased to consider ourselves the most democratic of all nations, but as a matter of fact, our Government is not as democratic as the Governments of Great Britain, France, Italy and others. I have tried to explain why in "Philip Dru", and I have also tried to present a really responsive form of government. It has been my purpose to show how our laws could be simplified so as to become understandable, and our courts rendered more effective, and stripped of their power to obstruct.

In order to bring about composure between capital and labor, some plan like Dru's might be tried, for, surely, our present method is a failure.

The tendancy [sic] of the times is to give more power to the executive of a state, for only in this way can efficient and economical government be reached. But in placing such power in the hands of one individual, the wise and cautious thing to do is to make the duration of the term of office subject to the will of the popular legislative body. Otherwise, great danger to the state may conceivably result.

The negative form of our Government has at times caused the President to assume almost dictatorial powers in order to bring about desired legislation, and the people of the United

States have accepted this assumption without protest. It is the executive part of the Government, both in the States and Nation, that almost always has the sympathy of the public, while the legislative side is generally ridiculed and belittled. In this way the already too great powers of the President have become augmented, and there have been no corresponding checks upon it.

It is true that in foreign affairs the Senate has sometimes refused to entirely accept the President's recommendations regarding treaties, but in the most pronounced instances it has been when the opposition party was in control and the issue became more a matter of politics than of policy.

Dru, in his plan of governmental reconstruction, tried to prevent these periodical hiatuses which must occur in such a government of negation as ours. It is a tribute to the good sense and self restraint of the American people that we have passed through so may crises without serious harm, but it is not wise to leave these loop-holes for trouble which some day might bring disorder and revolution.

It is astounding that an intelligent people having universal franchise as a means to remedy matters are willing to move along year after year and not better their governmental conditions. Was not Hardy right when he told Dru that the people received as good government as they deserved?

As an example let us take the costly and unnecessary monetery [sic] panics which swept over the United States at such frequent periods. No other country in the world had them and it was obvious that our banking and currency laws were at fault. It was not necessary to have any prescience in order to be able to frame a law which would correct the trouble, for we had the existing laws in Great Britain, France, Germany, Canada and other commercial nations to guide us. And yet we continued our wasteful and costly system for fifty years without changing it. What are we to say of a people who are so indifferent to their self-interest when it touches public affairs?

Those who were responsible for the Federal Reserve Act have recieved [sic] much commendation for securing its passage, but such commendation should be purely relative as it was the obvious thing to do. Would it not be more to the point if the people blamed themselves and those who were in power before who failed to do their obvious duty. [sic]

Governmental power has become so largely invested in the executive that only measures which he recommends and back of which he puts the strength of his office, have much chance of becoming laws. And the executive as a rule, is so busy with the day's work that he has but little time, and little inclination, to initiate legislation not on his party's program.

At no time should there be deadlocks between the Executive and Legislative branches of our Government. The one which occurred between President Wilson and the Senate has had disastrous consequences not alone to us but to the entire world. The future historian may well reckon that quarrel as one of the great tragedies that have befallen mankind. The consequences have gone far beyond the limits anticipated by the chief actors in it. It halted the most promising epoch in human history, and changed an expectant and exalted fervor in behalf of universal peace and good fellowship, into a spirit of sullen and cynical distrust.

It not only changed a hopeful world into a skeptical world, but its effect permeated the economic structure to an unbelievable degree. Industries have slackened when the waste from the Great War should have accelerated them; debts have piled upon debts, and millions of unhappy men, women and children have needlessly starved or died from preventable deseases.

[sic] It is a terrible reckoning and one which could not have occurred had our legislative and executive system of government been so constructed as to make impossible such a deadlock.

It might well be claimed that it should have been impossible even as it was, but when the baser human passions are aroused as then, it is wise and prudent not to have governmental machinery convenient through which such passions can be safely and constitutionally exercised.

The trouble with the world is that it never learns. We go blindly on making the same mistakes which those preceeding us have made. We listen to the sophistry of the eloquent self-seeker, and turn a dull ear to the blunt honesty of those not given to flattery or fluent speech. The demoagogue [sic] with his extravagant promises has his followers, just as the swindler has his victims. Something is seldom gotten for nothing, and that is a lesson many of us learn too late. If we are to prepare for old age or retirement, we must needs be [sic] frugal, energetic and painstaking. If we are to have good government we must be vigilent [sic] and willing to devote some of our time to its accomplishment. Philip Dru will have served his purpose if he has awakened even a small portion of his countrymen to a realization of this fact.

Index

About Robert Welch University Press ...

This new edition of *Philip Dru: Administrator* is the premier book-length publication of Robert Welch University Press. To gain an appreciation of the genre of material planned for RWU Press, we first direct the reader's attention to the remarks of William Norman Grigg in the "Foreword" to this edition. We find *Philp Dru* described as being an essential part of any political science student's collection of "political works which are read primarily for precautionary reasons" and as being "a successor to Machiavelli's essay *The Prince*."

The administrators of RWU Press do not take lightly the responsibility of making revealing studies of this caliber readily available to all students, instructors, and devotees of political science and public affairs. (Or at least to those sufficiently inspired to approach these studies from a perspective of true intellectual fervor and curiosity.)

In selecting titles for publication, the editors of RWU Press shall be guided by a philosophy of respect for intellectual, historical, and ethical truth — rather than by the current trend of "political correctness." For the former is perennial, the latter is transitory.

"There is one thing a professor can be absolutely certain of," noted University of Chicago professor Allan Bloom in *The Closing of the American Mind*, "almost every student entering the university believes, or says he believes, that truth is relative.... The relativity of truth is not a theoretical insight but a moral postulate, the condition of a free society, or so they see it. They have all been equipped with this framework early on, and it is the modern replacement for the inalienable natural rights that used to be the traditional American grounds for a free society.... Openness used to be the virtue that permitted us to seek the good by using reason. It now means accepting everything and denying reason's power." It is "not a means to exploring different answers to the great questions, but an excuse not to try to answer them at all."

Robert Welch University Press will not flee from its self-assigned mission to explore "different answers to the great questions."

The most pressing question of all, in the context of American society on the eve of the Twenty-first Century, is: How can we preserve, defend, and export America's greatest commodity: a legacy of political freedom in which all other freedoms — cultural, religious, economic, and academic — will flourish?

Celebrities — great — fred c turns